Special Praise for *The Blessing of Sorrow*

"Whether one is a person of deep faith or no faith, *The Blessing of Sorrow: Turning Grief into Healing* offers invaluable help to anyone dealing with the death of a loved one. It is a beautiful reflection on life—practical, down-to-earth, and compassionate for those grieving and who need light to find the way through the darkness of loss. As a Catholic parish priest for more than forty years, I highly recommend Rabbi Kamin's remarkable opus not only for the grieving, but also for those who minister to them in their hour of need."

Msgr. Dennis L. Mikulanis, STD, Pastor
Director of Diocesan Cemeteries of the Roman
Catholic Diocese of San Diego

"My heart is full as I finished reading *The Blessing of Sorrow*, a gentle and insightful look into healing from grief. Having experienced a gamut of grief and loss personally along with my professional experience as a midwife to the dying (hospice chaplain), I recognize a heart of compassion in Rabbi Kamin and felt immensely comforted, supported, understood, and honored to share in his journey. Whether you have just lost a loved one or desire more insight and support, this book will offer you a bridge to finding peace."

Corinne Cherek, M.Msc., BCC
Spiritual Counselor
Las Vegas Recovery Center Family Services

"Throughout his career, Rabbi Ben Kamin has officiated at numerous memorial services and comforted countless people—of all ages—along their journey with grief. He has seen the blessing of sorrow emerge when the grief was embraced and processed. This is a powerful, personal book that offers a sound and reasonable theological, psychological, and practical guide to bereavement. Read how to experience the loss of a loved one and eventually to experience joy and peace again."

Marjorie Foster Coburn, PhD
Psychologist

The Blessing of Sorrow

THE
BLESSING
OF
···· SORROW ····
Turning *Grief* into *Healing*

BEN KAMIN

CENTRAL RECOVERY PRESS

LAS VEGAS

Central Recovery Press (CRP) is committed to publishing exceptional materials addressing addiction treatment, recovery, and behavioral healthcare topics.

For more information, visit www.centralrecoverypress.com.

Publisher: Central Recovery Press
3321 N. Buffalo Drive
Las Vegas, NV 89129

23 22 21 20 19 18   1 2 3 4 5

Library of Congress Cataloging-in-Publication Data
Names: Kamin, Ben, author.
Title: The blessing of sorrow : turning grief into healing / Ben Kamin.
Description: Las Vegas : Central Recovery Press, [2018]
Identifiers: LCCN 2018000803 (print) | LCCN 2018013673 (ebook) |
ISBN 9781942094661 (ebook) | ISBN 9781942094654 (pbk. : alk. paper)
Subjects: LCSH: Grief. | Bereavement--Religious aspects. |
Death--Psychological aspects.
Classification: LCC BF575.G7 (ebook) | LCC BF575.G7 K36 2018 (print) | DDC
296.7/6--dc23
LC record available at https://lccn.loc.gov/2018000803

Author photo by *Photos by Solange* in San Diego, CA. Used with permission.

Every attempt has been made to contact copyright holders. If copyright holders have not been properly acknowledged please contact us. Central Recovery Press will be happy to rectify the omission in future printings of this book.

Publisher's Note: This book contains general information about grief, death and dying, spirituality, religious traditions, and related matters. The information is not medical advice. This book is not an alternative to medical advice from your doctor or other professional healthcare provider.

Our books represent the experiences and opinions of their authors only. Every effort has been made to ensure that events, institutions, and statistics presented in our books as facts are accurate and up-to-date.

Author's Note: Except in cases involving public figures, all names have been changed unless otherwise noted.

Cover design by The Book Designers. Interior design by Deb Tremper, Six Penny Graphics.

In memory of my father
Jeff I. Kamin

"Happiness is beneficial for the body, but it is grief that develops the powers of the mind."
Marcel Proust

Table of Contents

· · · · · · · · · · ·

The Ten Commandments of Grief

. . . .

1. Do not defer your sorrow; grieve openly, directly, and immediately.

2. Do not submit to any formula; grief is personal and a function of family history.

3. At the same time, accede to the stages of grief as they manifest themselves to you.

4. Turn to religious rituals that appeal to you and help you honor your loved one, but not simply because the rituals exist.

5. Encourage loved ones to *preplan* their funerals (you do the same) so that the inevitable grief is not further complicated by indecision or lack of direction.

6. Do not feel guilty if you feel relief that someone is no longer suffering.

7. Be discriminating when dealing with funeral directors. Most are commendable but even the best among them are nonetheless business professionals.

8. Do not hesitate to curtail memorial visits from even well-meaning people; you are entitled to rest and privacy and true friends will understand this.

9. Go back to work and play when you are ready and not because some old liturgical calendar dictates when you should.

10. Remember your dead as they plainly were; do not make them larger in death than they were in life.

Introduction

Do Not Defer Your Sorrow

· · · · · · · · · · ·

"The world breaks everyone and afterwards
many are strong at the broken places."
Ernest Hemingway

You are likely reading this book because someone close to you has died and you are grieving. Or perhaps someone beloved is dying and you are apprehensive and confused. You are in disbelief and don't know how to manage your anguish, your fears, and the strange feelings of anger that sometimes flash through you. The sorrow festers and haunts you. It sometimes takes control over you. You don't recognize your own behavior. One moment, you welcome the swell of people who come over to your home with sympathy, food, and many kind words about your dear one. The next moment you have no patience for anyone; you wish they'd all stop asking how you're doing and just go away. You want to be alone. You don't want to be alone. Your grief gnaws at your stomach and anxiety strangles your voice. You can barely breathe as the pain burrows deep into your mind, your body, and your soul.

An old photograph, a dog-eared book, a mug, a chair, or even a familiar hairbrush sends you into convulsions of sobbing and despair. Souls leave fingerprints. You gasp and struggle to push down the flutters of panic that suddenly appear and practically stop your heart. Death is harsh and final and terrifying and we Americans are not so adept at handling it or discerning the curative significance of grief. We often just turn over our bereavement to the clergy, the mortuaries, and even the radio and television psychologists who do the consoling, the business managing of the mortuary services, and the proffering of guidance. They do the work; we do the sadness.

Grief is a personal opportunity and, if dealt with directly, evolves into a hard-won blessing. Grief is a chance to visit with somebody at exactly the time he or she leaves you. Grief is a continued relationship with the dead that can nurture you rather than destroy you. This book is not about theology or clinical therapy in the matter of bereavement— although both play major roles for a lot of people when it comes to recovery from loss and death. Rather, this book is about helping people cross the bridge of grief to the path of peace. It does so less with religious sanctimony and more with real stories of people who have died well and left behind wiser survivors. Throughout these pages I'll not only share about learning how to live with loss but also the hope and promise found on the other side of the existence we know.

This book is based on my decades of comforting both the dying and their survivors, and contains a simple plea: however you do it, you *must* grieve. After all, grief and grieving are part of the human condition. If you put if off or avoid it altogether, you may suffer a delayed depression or a paralyzing melancholy as you attempt to return to your everyday activities. I've seen it happen too many times. It darkens your spirit and will threaten or cripple your ability to live, work, and play. That's not what your loved one wanted to happen to you. Let's not give more away to death than it has already taken.

In the spring of 2017, Britain's Prince Harry, one of the two surviving sons of Princess Diana, spoke publicly about mental health issues he suffered after deferring his grief. Harry declared he experienced "total chaos" and realized he was in need of professional help and intervention after some twenty years of shutting off his emotions and anguish. Diana died in August of 1997 in an automobile accident in Paris.

Harry stated, "My way of dealing with it was sticking my head in the sand, refusing to ever think about my mum, because why would that help. And then [I] started to have a few conversations and actually all of a sudden, all of this grief that I have never processed started to come to the forefront and I was like, there is actually a lot of stuff here that I need to deal with."[1]

The human body and soul were designed to heal. We recuperate from many illnesses and we mend from broken bones. But what greater anguish is there than a heart broken by grief? I once put off a certain grief for months and then found myself crashing into the hole of a biological and situational depression that required therapies, medications, acupuncture, endless support from friends, and my own will to live in order to recover. The body-soul is a holistic essence, and it does not compromise with us when we try to deceive it about an embedded and unresolved bereavement. When the depression consumed me, my life hurt day and night. Getting through the performance of my professional duties and even social experiences all felt like an out-of-body experience. I slipped into a dark dance with despair. Grief is not a distraction; it is a provisional emotional melanoma that settles into our bodies and literally disrupts the neurons of our brains.

I have learned—and I have witnessed—that when we lean into the grief and embrace its pain, it can become part of the cure and it will develop into a blessing. When we submit to it, which requires courage and endurance, it will build an open passageway between our beloved and us for all times. But this can only happen if we do not circumvent the grieving or defer it or pretend it is negotiable or passable. Only when

1 http://www.independent.co.uk/news/uk/home-news/prince-harry-counselling-death-of-princess-diana-mental-health-issues-a7686786.html.

we accede to it does it, in time, build a bridge that connects heaven to earth. To paraphrase Anthony Lane of the *New Yorker*, there is "a dance to the music of grief."[2]

Death is a mighty and fearsome event and it can trigger chronic despondency, bottomless sorrow, guilt, regrets, and psychological dysfunction. However you handle it, bereavement cannot be dispensed with glib gestures or perfunctory rituals. It is hard work. Grief is the ultimate partnership between gentleness and suffering. If you do not confront it directly, you will find yourself in the abyss of loneliness within any given time.

There are several things to learn about how to grieve: Why and how is bereavement a necessary and healing transition? Why is it detrimental to bypass or suspend it? Is there really a "right way" to experience it? Does it require religious ceremonials or is it ultimately a private, spiritual journey? Or is the answer perhaps somewhere in between? How do we carry on with life itself after someone's death? Does the personal passage of grief ultimately inform our lives and make us better people, more able to understand and service the pain of others?

Forty years after my father's death, bereavement is the centerpiece of my rabbinate, the privilege I cherish the most, and I work with people of all faiths and traditions. I wish to help those who are trapped in grief because each one of us eventually becomes such a person. Rationalizing or simplifying the trauma of losing someone can irretrievably damage both body and mind. Grief cannot be suspended.

Bereavement is life's most life-enlightening transition. I hope you find comfort in my words as you mourn, remember, and make peace with your journey of grief.

---

2 Anthony Lane, The Current Cinema, "Jackie" and "Allied," the *New Yorker*, (December 5, 2016).

Chapter One

Grief Is Personal: Is There Any One Way to Grieve?

· · · · · · · · · · ·

"There is no grief like the grief that does not speak."
Henry Wadsworth Longfellow

Let's face it: we suffer dreadfully when someone we love dies. In the New Testament, Christians read about "the sting of death." Jews recite, "So teach us to number our days that we may grow a heart of wisdom." An old Islamic proverb declares, "Do not sit idle, for indeed death is seeking you." And the Buddha asserts, "There is no blissful peace until one passes beyond the agony of life and death." It doesn't matter if someone is devoutly religious or agnostic or atheist or seeks spirituality through contemplative meditation, as humans it is only natural that we tend to fret about our mortality and suffer when someone dear to us dies.

Yet Americans are generally not comfortable or expressive with our grief. We're a talkative, fun-loving, youth-worshipping people who are remarkably reticent and evasive about the direst yet most common thing that ever happens to us: losing a parent, a sibling, a child, a spouse, a partner, a friend. And dying is unequivocally the one thing each and every one of us will do—regardless of creed, philosophies, or social circumstances.

Meanwhile, the media and the internet have effectively sanitized death. Death has become a celebrity on CNN and other news outlets where we see people executed and tortured into lifelessness. War and acts of terrorism are telecast day and night, and it is standard for us to behold images of dying or murdered individuals. Or we watch people simply and serenely passing away in a hospital bed during a television or cinematic drama. It becomes difficult—especially for young people— to distinguish between reality and cybernetics and this trivializes the unforgiving truths about death and dying.

There are few, if any, programs or presentations about survivors and how they suffer and adjust and cope and hopefully recover from these traumas. People are shown dying in movies but rarely does the screenplay show a lot of people grieving.

How We Grieve

When my father died suddenly at the age of forty-five in the spring of 1976, my young mother and my two siblings and me were shocked, confused, angry, and afflicted with a sense of abandonment. His funeral would be the first I ever attended. I was twenty-three. Just prior to the service, my mother elected to take a private "last look" at her lifetime sweetheart. She was escorted behind a curtain into a room where he lay in a plain pine box. I could hear her crying out his name over and over again in between bursts of muffled screams.

I couldn't do it. I couldn't go into the room to see my dead father. I wanted to remember him vigorous, dynamic, and full of his trademark passion. Death is personal and there are no set rules on how to grieve, regardless of the devotionals that appear in myriad clergy manuals.

Many of us Americans are caught between our fear and denial of death, our discomfort with the subject of mortality, and the guilt imposed by some religious traditions when it comes to "doing the correct thing." I don't have an argument with the organized faiths. I simply prefer to service grieving families at their point of need and without pretending they are religiously observant if they actually are not. When someone dies, he or she should be memorialized in the way he or she lived and believed. Death is an aspect of life, not a liturgical opportunity.

I have performed countless memorial ceremonies since that harsh and revealing milestone of my father's demise. I still see his bulky figure covered under a sheet on a handball court the night he collapsed. There was blood off to the side; he succumbed so intensely to a massive heart attack that the rim of his eyeglasses cut into his forehead. Paramedics, police, and bystanders walked and talked quietly in the little court as I stared at my father's sneakers, which stuck out from under the sheet.

I am well acquainted with the delicate handiwork, nuances, contradictions, and failures associated with bereavement in America. We don't always reminisce well; we transfer our angst into emotional burlesque because we are raised in a video culture that does not train us to lament. Years ago, an Alabama mortuary initiated "drive-thru" visitation that allowed people to pull up in their automobiles, stop, and view the remains of a deceased loved one in an open casket through a glass window. Here was the original archetype of the American-style fast-food funeral: coping with and honoring the dead became the requiem-equivalent of an ATM transaction.

The father of psychoanalysis, Sigmund Freud, writing from Vienna, once backhandedly and unflatteringly compared how Americans and Europeans conceptualize the bereavement process. He was alerting the bereaved not to depreciate the grieving process: if not respected and experienced, "it becomes as hollow and empty as an American flirtation in which it is understood from the beginning that nothing is to happen, in contrast to a continental [European] love affair in which both partners must always bear in mind the serious consequences."[3]

3 Sigmund Freud, *Reflections on War and Death* (New York: Moffat, Yard, and Company, 1918).

I ask: Why fear death? You are going back to the same place you were before you were born. Do you fear that place? It was but a peaceful void. You were invulnerable to any agony or distress. To not exist is to not suffer and to not bear burdens. When people die, grieve for them fully but then let them go. Nothing else from this life can happen to them.

And nothing clarifies the fact that we are all simply human beings more than the universal denominator of mortality. A cemetery is a field of souls and there is no theology planted in its grasses and hills, only the tenderness of memory. A common practice in a communal cemetery is to maintain Jewish, Christian, and Muslim sections. I respect that, but I don't believe land can be divvied up doctrinally. I admire the Native American philosophy that the earth is as whole and as unbound as the sky. The earth has no liturgy but its silence. Grief is the completed language of life.

When my father died, my family was suddenly faced with the questions every family or individual deals with at such a time. What do we do? When should the service take place? Should we follow religious procedures or not? Where do we have the service? Should it perhaps simply be a graveside ceremony? (My young father did not make these kinds of arrangements in advance with something the funeral conglomerates call "pre-needs.")

In our case, there was no question my dad would be interred—the very next day. We belonged to an Orthodox synagogue, requiring burial within twenty-four hours. The cemetery experience was a walk through numbness and barely comprehended emotions. It remains a blurred memory for me. It failed to initiate the therapy of grief. It was just a series of recitations and obligatory actions all set to a twenty-four-hour clock. We followed a somber doctrinal formula that serviced our need to lay my father to rest, but it did nothing to address our emotions and agony.

Many families struggle today in a different way—particularly in this society of constant choices and unfettered options. Should it be a burial or a cremation? Or perhaps some alternative method or venue should be considered? In America, even death has been conjoined to the entertainment and youth cultures. It shouldn't be too sad—maybe it could be even a little entertaining. And customary funerals are known to be very costly.

I have labored side-by-side with people in the funeral industry for a long time. Most of them are earnest, meticulous individuals who regard their work with gravitas and display high standards. They listen carefully to the family members they serve, are attentive to unusual requirements and special requests, and speak gently and with an appropriate level of pastoral kindness. From day to day—and sometimes in the middle of the night—they interact with a gamut of distraught human beings who are reacting to somebody's death in all variety of ways, some rational and others erratic and volatile.

It's all bewildering and confusing because in the United States, bereavement is much more successful as a business for mortuaries, casket companies, and cemetery properties than it is therapy for deeply sorrowful and needy survivors. We just don't commiserate much about death. About forensics and murders we are saturated with media and documentaries. Anti-aging ointments and vanity treatments to artificially recreate youth are rampant. We rarely consider the stern mental health consequences of avoiding grief because we much prefer youth and vitality, and we too often simply dispatch our aging and dying parents to hospitals or "old age homes"—where they finish their lives in the hands of skilled, caregiving strangers and mostly out of our view.

Funerals and Bereavement Practices

As in any enterprise, there are unfortunate exceptions among these people and there are a few trends that betray the "bottom-line" aspect of the business. Some funeral marketers might pitch you a sailboat-shaped coffin, replete with the contour of a hull and a rudder if Dad was a mariner—one of several, new-wave, amusing, pricey, theme-based alternative burial boxes. One funeral home I worked with for many years maintained a special display in its Casket Room—a Marsellus 710 mahogany casket that was elegant and had a brownish stain and semi-gloss finish. "This is the exact same model of casket that President Kennedy was buried in," the service adviser would tell mourners.

Or you can go online to order what is advertised as a "fan-based" *Star Trek* coffin, embellished with all the graphics in color. The site selling this model as well as a *Grand Theft Auto* unit declares that the *Star Trek* casket "will not get old." You can sign on to eBay and personally order a "RARE Antique Child's Burial Casket Coffin Pine Wood Box Colonial New York City." The list price in 2016 was $1,495.95. These unique last resting places may offer a bit of whimsy during an inconsolable time; however, I feel they offer little dignity and negligible clinical recuperation. Maybe it's one reason an inside joke among some funeral executives is that the first three letters of funeral spell "fun."

The whole funeral culture is a rather sad symptom of why, in 2016, *Time* magazine termed America as "a radical democracy of personal choice." While there are important options and methods involving grief, what's sometimes lost upon many of us is that there are no options *not* to grieve. We can choose what condiments we want on our fast-food hamburgers or what luxury features we prefer in our new automobile, but there is no poll about death. It is absolutely certain.

Today's sometimes-outlandish bereavement practices didn't originate in the Hebrew Scripture. They are the products of American mercantilism. In Genesis, we read that Sarah, the wife of Abraham, dies. The Bible then tells us, simply, "And Abraham came to cry for her, mourn for her, and eulogize her." That's it. No frills, devices, add-ons, or commercial gimmicks. The widower unpretentiously wept (a good message for men who are reluctant to shed tears in public), lamented, and told her life story—the first record of a eulogy in biblical literature. This was the beginning of an eventual emotional recovery because Abraham took hold of his pain immediately and naturally. And he spoke about it.

Recovering emotionally through fulfilled grieving is a significant issue in the medical community. Physicians in America are not encouraged to cry or display their anguish; it's considered a sign of weakness or helplessness that is not tolerated by some peers. Depression, dysfunction, and even suicide are more common than generally known. One doctor wrote:

> In medicine, crying is unprofessional. That needs to change—now. A premedical student volunteering in the local ER tells me about a female physician who cried after losing a child. He thought her behavior was unprofessional. I asked him to consider "Who did she harm by crying?" Meanwhile, a physician tells me she's been cited for unprofessional conduct for crying at work. Her boss told her, "Unless you are dying, crying is unprofessional behavior and not to be tolerated." Some physicians and young doctors-in-training are uncomfortable with tears. Grieving is a healthy reaction to sadness. Humans bond through shared pain. Please do not punish your colleagues for their willingness to be vulnerable with grief-stricken families. Real doctors cry.[4]

Today, the potentially sanitizing term "a celebration of life" is used in place of memorial or funeral, and is often dictated by family members. I always honor the request because I have respect for people's sensibilities. But I retain some concerns about this phrase. I have conducted memorials in places as disparate as hotel ballrooms, bars,

4 Dr. Pamela Wible writing on the website, KevinMD.com. http://www.kevinmd.com/blog/2015/03/why-did-this-image-of-a-crying-doctor-go-viral-heres-why.htm.

arboretums, zoological gardens, picnic parks, along the seashore, at home, and, of course, in chapels and at graveside ceremonies.

Regardless of the location or method of sending a loved one to eternity, no matter what music is played, slide shows presented, or what the eulogists say or forget to say, most every funeral ends the same way: the grievers, in injured stillness, go home to a contorted world as the house fills up with overflowing platters of food and the strangely melancholy aroma of brewing coffee. For the newly bereaved, the menu is loneliness and, though people encircle them, they suffer quietly like soulless outcasts.

Grief is the emotional blood that must circulate through the body and be cleansed by the spiritual yearnings that inhabit our psyches. There is no definitive approach just as there is no one particular way to lead a life. One unusual practice—formerly evident among French Jews—is a compelling paradigm of how to weave grief effectively into the tapestry of everyday life.

The Table of Life

A tradition in some French-Jewish communities was for the men to construct a table from any good and suitable wood that would be used for family gatherings and on which to enjoy their meals. Each man would do so knowing that his coffin would one day be built from the wood of that very table. I think about this custom from time to time— especially in twenty-first-century America, where sorrow and mourning are rarely discussed or planned for.

Picture the imagery: a man's family and friends come to his funeral and see his casket, which was once the table where they had sat and talked and laughed and cried. Grief is therapeutic and healing when it has handprints all over our lives, when it is part of the subconscious long before it comes along with its pain and desolation.

The origin of this table-to-coffin notion, found in the Talmud, is that since the Jews no longer had the Temple in Jerusalem—it was destroyed by the Romans in 70 CE—"a person receives atonement through his table." The kitchen table is where a person can give nourishment to others, invite the poor to come and eat, bless family members, and generally share his or her bounty and good fortune. Or it can be the center of emotional indigestion and spiritual hunger. As plates are filled and conversations ensue, souls mingle or bump into each other most directly. You learn a lot about people who will eventually die, after the days and evenings spent around the tabletop. You will have tender details to remember—the shape of their hands, their trademark fragrance, a piece of music they hummed, classic phrases they repeatedly invoked—thus keeping them spiritually alive.

Most of us can recall the kitchen table of our childhood and adolescence. Stories were told, anger was flashed, quarrels were resolved, or people broke up with each other and someone left the table in a huff. We saw and heard our parents up-close and without ceremony; they cajoled one another, interrogated us kids, declared rules, expressed their love, bickered about finances, and they certainly disciplined us. It wasn't always congenial but it was real and some things spoken there have never been forgotten. The table was a kind of sanctuary of personal history. The table is still the landscape of truths, sullen and blissful.

What you do and say at the kitchen table, how you behave, how you degrade or inspire others, become the etchings of other people's memory and the libretto of their grief when you die. One's eulogy is inscribed over the years in the clanking plates and cutlery, the steaming soups, the briskets or tofu-turkeys, the exceptionally celebrated maternal entrees, the romantic anecdotes, the generational stories, the weeping, the shouting, and the forgiving. Even the matter of who prepares the meal and how the table is set define the rhythm of real life in a household.

It wasn't always pleasant at the meals, but it was tangible and some things spoken there have never been discarded. Converting the table's wood into a coffin eternalized the nuances of a human being and serviced the mourners who, at the funeral, literally beheld the same planks around which they had sat for decades. It was not about the mortuary or the formulaic obituary or the lofty tributes of designated speakers. It was certainly not about how long or ornate was the table of someone's life. It was about what the table was made of.

So wherever this practice prevailed, the builder of the table, chopping and refining the wood, designing the pattern, smoothing the corners, knew from the start that he was also creating a legacy derived from the exact lumber of his efforts.

In the end, life and death evolve from the trunks and branches of the same tree. There is a protecting shade about grief and—if bereavement is anticipated and contemplated—it will provide us with the fruit and nourishment of healing. We start with the realization that there can be no tree of life without a seed being planted. Grief and memory are the natural alchemy that renews the table of life even after someone has left it.

A Righteous Deed

The requisite and pressing group of relatives and friends crowd the house, eating, drinking, and awkwardly uttering clichés ("He'll be missed"; "She is in a better place"). Most people do mean well and try to say something sincerely felt. But it's ultimately a social gathering, because we Americans—who know so much about sex, politics, good wine, travel, the movies, and the National Football League—just don't know how to talk about death. It's as if we have embraced what Epicurus said in the fourth century BCE, "Death does not concern us, because as long as we exist, death is not here." We really have the tendency to simply dismiss death for as long as possible even though it is life's absolute equal. Then, to our amazement, it is here.

When at a house of mourning, some visitors will seek a bit of solace as they engage in conversations about a variety of banal subjects. Avoiding the obvious situation, they prattle about the news, the stock market, their kids' soccer championship, and, of course, the weather. When you are a mourner, you are allowed to let people know that you are too tired for any further conversation. You do not need permission to graciously announce you are done and are going to bed.

The most beneficial and remedial gatherings at home after a funeral involve mostly silence. People sitting together, offering few words but generally keeping quiet, transmit the strongest and certainly the most honest message. We are here. We care.

Don't get me wrong. There is real consolation in having people around after the trauma of a burial and they should be welcomed and thanked. People just have to think about how to visit well. It's not a get-together; it's a righteous deed. Because soon enough the hardest part comes for the bereaved: the last guests leave, the door shuts for the last time, and the survivors or the individual suddenly widowed find themselves in a terrible new darkness. There is his toothbrush sitting in its slot on the sink. Her dresses and shoes hang and lie forlorn in the closet. There is a gaping absence in the bed where he would lie and sleep every night. Even the abandoned pillow seems to be weeping.

Inside a Terrible New Darkness

This might be the loneliest moment in someone's life. None of the kindly or just meandering talk with all the visitors really relieved anything—even in its sincerity. There is but a hole in our hearts—we who have been thrust into bereavement.

French novelist Colette wrote, "It's so curious: one can resist tears and 'behave' very well in the hardest hours of grief. But then someone makes you a friendly sign behind a window, or one notices that a flower that was in bud only yesterday has suddenly blossomed, or a letter slips from a drawer . . . and everything collapses."[5]

After the house or the reception hall empties, the family members are left with the gnawing, sometimes debilitating, acutely painful realization, "I don't know what to do. Should I be stoic and just carry on? Should I just stay home and weep for several days? When should I return to work? How many days away from everything are appropriate? Should I turn to prayers and ceremonials that I really am not familiar with? Shall I seek out clinical help or join a support group?

In the case of my father, I got some help with my anguish—not from the rabbi who spoke at his burial and confused my father's first name with mine, and not from a therapist or grief counselor (although these are essential professionals, many of them extremely proficient and wise, who can drive the necessary process of real grieving). My religion offered rituals that were ancestrally soothing (a daily service every evening in our home for a week; covered mirrors; small, stiff seats for us mourners; memorial candles; the inevitable, endless trays of deli) but I soon got two better remedies that launched my recovery. The first was a solo walk in a park, and later, a visit from my astute uncle, who arrived from Israel.

A day or so after the house had emptied of callers and the emptiness began to fill our home like a gloomy fog, I got into my car and began to drive. I found myself at a familiar, hilly, and verdant public park. French Park began as a private estate in the early 1900s. It had the family mansion, thick woods, endless meadows and trails, and was a regular gathering place for my chums and me during our high school years. My dad favored it for an occasional family picnic; he and I would often hike along its creeks and under dogwoods, elms, and buckeyes, discussing

5 Colette, *Letters from Colette* (New York: Random House, 1983), 61.

life, my future, and his work as an aerospace engineer during those early, heady days of manned space flight.

My grief spilled into the shrubs and Japanese roses more naturally than it had during the daily, book-bound mourning prayers at the synagogue with my younger brother, and certainly more unreservedly than at the house teeming with concerned friends. I could see my dad and me throwing a baseball back and forth in this park during earlier, happier spring times. I could hear him calling us kids back from the nearby thicket and announcing that the hot dogs were ready while ordering me to open up the cooler with the Coca-Colas. I could see his thick, dark, curly hair that would never be streaked with gray because he died so young.

I arrived at French Park's popular shelter, where parties were often thrown. Mercifully, today it was all my own. A forgiving breeze filled up the space and I thought I detected the pleasant scent of my father's trademark Mennen "Afta" aftershave lotion. The shelter became my synagogue.

I smiled through my sorrow and tears and felt the first layer of release. I looked up at the deep blue April sky and saw a formation of puffy clouds and my father's profile forming in the clean white swirls. It didn't matter to me whether it was a real, heavenly gesture or simply the product of my bittersweet yearnings. What mattered to me was that I was releasing something—something uninhibited, not accountable to any formula, undistracted by protocols—and I actually visited with my departed dad.

That was the day I first discovered how to grieve.

The next day, Uncle Moshe arrived for a three-month stay.

Moshe was my mother's older brother and had always been a very close comrade of my father. The entire clan hails from Israel, where I was born. The two men fought side-by-side in Israel's War of Independence and Moshe, chain-smoking, gravelly voiced, opinionated, and extremely adoring of his entire family circle, looked something like an Israeli version of Tevye the Dairyman. He was no stranger to death, having killed men in war and witnessed many of his childhood friends and fellow soldiers slaughtered. He had little use for religion, but was a pragmatist who believed instead in solid, manual work and keeping an open door for his children and his friends. He was unquestionably the family patriarch.

On the night my father died, my mother called Moshe in Ashdod, Israel, and asked him to fly over to us in Cincinnati and spend a few weeks with us.

"I'm on my way," I heard him say over the telephone receiver, shaken to also hear him sobbing.

When Moshe arrived after taking his first-ever airplane excursion—he had spent his entire life as an infantryman and then as a bus driver—he found a traumatized family in need of a father figure. My sister was twelve years old and had danced among the nearby tombstones while we put my father into the ground. My brother, sixteen, had particularly idolized our father and emulated his athleticism and was emotionally immobilized. My mother, when she wasn't holding onto her big brother, regularly went into the kitchen and cried into the sink.

But I kept wondering, as so many bereaved do: *Where is my father now?*

Two or three nights after his arrival, Moshe invited me to take a walk under the stars. He was never a particularly reverential man, but felt things intensely. He did not attempt to disguise his grief; it weaved its way into his weatherworn face, moistened his deep dark eyes, and occasionally caused his normally powerful voice to crack. But there was some kind of peace, walking with just him, on that balmy night of shadows laced with the fragrance of the springtime geraniums. Looking skyward while pacing alongside my uncle, I recalled something I once read in a prayer book: "The stars are there even when you can't see them in the daytime."

"Are you looking at heaven?" Moshe asked me with tenderness.

"I suppose I am," I replied, as he put his arm around me. His corduroy jacket emitted the familiar blend of tobacco and street wisdom.

"Your father and I used to do that many years ago as campfires burnt out during the war. The night stars were soothing to us because we feared death every day. We agreed they were the lights of heaven. I felt closer to that idea out there in the Samarian Mountains than at any of the times I ever went into a synagogue."

The exchange, more mystical than usual for Moshe, prompted me to ask the question that plagued me the most since my father's abrupt death. I asked, "Moshe, where is my father?"

Moshe stopped walking, thought about it, while wrinkling his brow. A bit of a knowing smile on his face was evident under the starshine.

"Ben," he said, very deliberately. "I knew your father. And I can tell you that he's in a good place."

"But how do you know that?" I retorted.

"Tell me something." My uncle focused on me, soul to soul. "Your father was very particular and he didn't have patience for trivialities. So, if it wasn't a good place, don't you think he'd come back?"

This bit of raw theology has helped me over the years. I have shared the moment and the message with others from time to time when they were freshly bereaved and grappling with how to grieve—even with the liturgical rites, the psychotherapeutic sessions, and the consoling input of friends who knew how to just listen. Uncle Moshe's response and his conviction amounted to a measure of folk formulation; but it really was tender and intuitive. I was calmed by his roundabout way of telling me how much he loved my father. And the notion that my father would simply come back if he was unhappy has continued to give me a measure of comfort and a warm chuckle over the course of time.

Holding onto that little burst of hope, like my interlude at French Park, assisted me on the path of grief. It helped me to find a tender

location in my soul for my dad. Where is your loved one? Safely at
home—in your heart.

Grief Is Personal

For some forty years I've observed and listened carefully to people
while working in bereavement situations. I've appeared unannounced
at people's homes and informed them that someone they cherished died
or committed suicide or was killed. I've been present in hospitals and
hospices at the moment of death, embraced the family members, and
prayed with them. I've listened to their wailing and bewilderment and—
as standard practice—used an economy of words in response to their
questions of "why?"

I've stood by at the side of a swimming pool as a child was pulled
out lifeless from drowning. I've helped parents cut down their teenagers
from the nooses with which they killed themselves in their bedrooms
or garages. I've closed the eyes of men and women who expired from
gunshot wounds as they lay under bloodied sheets in emergency rooms
and "urgent care centers."

Grief is not a uniform experience. Like life, it's personal. People die
in widely dissimilar ways and at all ages. So we must keep in mind that
the circumstances of a death impact the manner in which people will
react and recover. I have rarely relied on gratuitous theological clichés
to rationalize their anguish. People just want to be heard and get their
torment out. Again, we goodhearted family and friends often talk too
much when confronting the fresh sorrow of others. They are the ones
who need to talk or scream and they actually appreciate the eloquence
of our more silent empathy.

The earth has opened at burials and mourners have clutched their
hearts over and over again. Some howl in agony; others feel too empty
to even shed tears. Sporadically, I've noticed a few people bursting out
with inexplicable laughter as though their psyche has been completely

unhinged by the situation. No one is ever really prepared for it, even if a departed parent had been ill for some time or had simply aged enough that life gave out.

No matter how old we are when our mother or our father dies, we are still simply their children. A piece of us dies with them. Some psychologists argue that it's even harder to lose a spouse.[6] With parents, a sense of emotional security evaporates. We recall how we depended upon them, how they made us feel safe, and reassured us by their presence that we would never be alone and vulnerable or even responsible for the family narrative. They took care of everything, the money, the places where we lived, the vacations, the bruises we endured physically and psychically from friends, neighbors, and even our schoolteachers. They were the authors of our family histories and they were never supposed to die.

Granted, they didn't always measure up, and there were conflicts and discords. We were sometimes disappointed with and fought bitterly with them. Guilt and unresolved anger weave their way into the grieving process like sinister threads of complication and perplexity. But our parents and our other elders simply being there were often like a warm sweater neutralizing the cold winds of our own mortality.

My experience has also instilled in me that while people leave us, their souls linger somewhere. I call bereavement "a song to creation." In other words, it is a healing protocol that weaves together the world we know and the world we fear. I am not a mystic. I am a rational, practicing rabbi who believes people must truly grieve in order to endure a death. However, that does not mean this life is all we know about what endures in the universe. I've undergone too many moments of transcendence to deny what no scientist can possibly prove—that life

---

6 I personally have observed that people suffer most grievously after losing a child, but don't think there is any definitive scientific conclusion here. To lose anyone you love is an immeasurably harsh reality.

is only what we see before us. Years ago, while alone with the deceased's closed casket, I heard the strains of his favorite Broadway musical softly emerge. My own father appeared to me just a few nights after his death in a particle of floating lights that filled me with peace.

This life was something that existed long before we came along with our geological calibrations, our stargazing and marine probes, and our evolutionary studies. It is something that cannot be posted on a technical list of universal components. The human soul does not appear with carbon, nitrogen, uranium, and helium on the chart of natural elements.

Science is the uneasy partner of theology but remains one of the most urgent quests on earth. The moon hangs and orbits in the sky and this can be explained with astrophysics. Men have landed there and walked on its surface. But the moon will always raise more lyrics from poets and romantics than it will provide evidential data to astronauts and technicians. We humans are drawn to mystery; it both inspires and terrifies us. Science is a series of rational unsympathetic questions waiting to be resolved, and it does not suffer nuances.

Both spiritualists and scientists agree that every person is born and every person dies. What happens before and what transpires afterward remain the most tantalizing, confounding, and unresolved matters of the human mind, inspiring verse, music, divinity, and a whole lot of anxiety.

No aspect of my ministry is more significant or edifying to me than my regular interaction with the dying and the dead and my obligations to their survivors. In both pastoral counseling and the actual sequences of death and burial, they have bequeathed me two precious results: I have no fear of my own death, and certain experiences have convinced me that there is some sort of afterlife.

Too many reasonable and thoughtful individuals—many of them non-religious or atheists—have shared their stories with me of reassuring and enriching visits from their departed loved ones. They didn't necessarily rhapsodize their recollections or grab my arm or even claim a special ecclesiastic vision. They normally didn't invoke scriptural references. They just spoke quietly and with serenity and told me things that helped me to affirm that we human beings, even with our vanities and cyber-clout, simply don't know everything about the path of the soul. So we are given to weeping, praying, hoping, and speculating. We also become emotionally vulnerable; especially in this digital world in which a cellular phone can be utilized to answer or resolve pretty much any inquiry. Except, that is, the finality of death.

The death of a loved one is a potential assault on one's mental health. Grief and depression are the darkly disabling partners that torment people who do not properly absorb and distill their sorrow. We have to find remedial and therapeutic ways to grieve when our elders, friends, and even children die, because they are gone from this world as far as we understand and perceive it. They are vanished from our kitchen tables and they are physically absent—and painfully missed— at the baptisms, bar mitzvah ceremonies, confirmations, and weddings that followed their passing. We miss them and, when suddenly replacing our parents as the leaders and role models at Christmas dinner or the Passover Seder, we feel the poignancy of our own advancing mortality and discover a queasy sadness and loneliness that is the bittersweet calendar of our existence. We don't like the way the deaths of our parents make us grow up.

We need to be cautious with the declaration that our dead are "in a better place." I feel this even with the heartening visit from my father. Some therapists believe it's a quick theological throwaway because people simply want to reallocate death via an old succor they've always heard and now mimic. Their concern is that uttering the cliché can create a distraction from the hard facts of a death and impede people from the grieving process.

I've heard colleagues moan that the phrase about "a better place" is a repudiation of *life itself* being the preeminent place—even when it tries, hurts, and ultimately grows us. But I do know, as a teacher of human life, and as someone who sees bereavement as a bridge between two worlds, that our dead are *someplace, somewhere.* Anyone who is in awe of creation (scientifically or doctrinally) cannot logically deem that we humans are created to simply rot away as though we had never existed. I don't believe in ghosts; I believe in souls. And I myself have seen, heard, and even smelled them coming and going.

I cannot count how many times I have officiated at funerals over the past forty years. The figure is certainly in the hundreds but the only meaningful number is one. One person, one death with a narrative, a faith or philosophy system, a heart that was alternately elated and broken, a set of talents, a flair for this or that, high hopes and irritating traits, an array of achievements, and a list of indiscretions or even crimes. Some had clean and lovely hands; some were missing fingers, a leg, an internal organ, or bore a physical deformity that affected his or her existence altogether. Some had died slowly of cancer or dementia while others were killed instantly by gunshot wounds or in automobile accidents. Some were ethically noble people, given to kindness and generosity; others were insufferable cranks who tested the patience of their family and friends or even damaged others' psyches with their own self-absorption or cruelty. When people die, they are still themselves, even with the elegiac window-dressing that attends many funerals. The persona of our departed guides us to the manner in which we grieve. We need to remember them the way they were: someone who was not religious, for example, need not be given a requiem filled with theological rituals. Let the dead be honored as they were.

Some people knew they were dying and displayed the kind of dignity that sent their bereft loved ones—their friends, protégés, or students—back to serve the living. We will surely meet such people.

Some were angry, difficult to help, and understandably frightened. Some turned decidedly mean and ungrateful. We were secretly relieved when they actually took their last breaths. Finally, peace, we thought. That reaction is normal and not some kind of a sin.

Not everyone is affirmative in life and, sadly, they can become oppressive in the process of dying. There is no filter for their demands, complaints, rage, and resentment—all driven by their understandable fears and already less-than-sunny personalities. Adding an irony to the mix is that we frequently soon come to miss these bad-tempered ones because in spite of their cantankerousness, they were the clockwork of our daily routines and now we feel useless and strangely empty. I have sensed at many funeral services that some of the mourners were feeling newly liberated while the caretakers, professionals, or family members—the ones who had changed the bedpans, administered the towel baths, and suffered the bile of the dying—had a different reaction. These good folks were truly overwhelmed with the discomfiting question: what will I do every day now?

There is much less to fear than we assume or suffer through. Souls do mingle with us in daily life and they have as much a spiritual presence in our lives as when our bodies were simply housing them while they were with us on this side.

A Life Remembered

The American relationship with death and dying could still benefit from maturation, more straight talk, and a lot less posturing. And in my case, how a sudden "nudge" from a soul I love and admire helped me to negotiate the bridge of bereavement.

I was present at this occasion termed a memorial service since there was no body or casket present. The phrase "memorial service" is often invoked rather than the term "funeral" in the case of a cremation or in an instance, like the one I attended, when the forensic specialists were still investigating the death. No matter. Many Americans are reticent about death and tend to sterilize it, regardless of the services that are selected. So this was one of those requiems we often compassionately declare, or rationalize, as "A Celebration of Life."

It is, no doubt, a heartening label, this "Celebration of Life"—sweet, soothing, and hopeful. It is a harvest of tenderness at a moment of dark lines and edgy realities, yet not without its weeds of denial. It is the voice of the child in each of us, a throwback to the time before people we knew and loved left us and now we find ourselves not totally equipped to handle the tyranny of mortality. So we compensate with florid speeches and with displays of light and homilies of praise that often avoid the woeful surrender to truth: somebody is dead and some day we will be, too.

Meanwhile, the life of the young father and husband being fêted was cut short by a dreadful swimming accident while he and his family were enjoying a holiday on a distant island far from their home in Southern California. The exact circumstances of the father's demise were still not established at the time of this lavish hotel memorial gathering almost three weeks after the calamity. His remains were not released and the island police and coroner were taking their time exploring the circumstances.

The only thing the numb family knew for sure was that Mitchell, a successful entrepreneur and avid globetrotter, was gone. Now it was time to gather a host of family members and friends and do something to mark the tragedy with a hotel gathering and a carefully choreographed humanistic service. A video biography, underscored with familiar pop ballads, played across two large screens as the well-heeled crowd filled the hall. *Alas, death is indifferent to shoes, purses, lipstick, double-breasted suits, and turbo-charged automobiles*, I thought to myself.

I was asked to moderate the occasion because Mitchell was Jewish (his wife and son are not). They were "spiritual, not religious"—an increasingly common designation, which, I think, adds to the inexplicit anxiety of these elaborate assemblages. Grief needs processing. It demands sorrowfulness and consolation. They requested very little Hebrew liturgy and appreciated my practice of making any life-cycle event that I lead inclusive and accessible.

"Make it upbeat, Rabbi," Mitchell's father told me. The older gentleman was sad; I could see it, but his face would simply not be broken by it. There were people to greet and friends to glad-hand and introductions to be remade among people who hadn't seen each other in a long time. Folks were talking but souls were not mingling. The rituals were strictly the beats and measures of a gossip culture and not a civilization that is informed by the authentic seasons of life.

The obvious was avoided as people walked in, wearing suits and sundresses, coiffed and generally not prepared to give in to tears. It was as though they had an unspoken agreement not to touch upon emotions. Attorneys, car dealers, stockbrokers, and real estate magnates mixed and caught up while sipping on the lemon-flavored cold water that flowed from two large crystal vessels. There was a kind of vague disbelief that clung to the room. It was as if nothing had really happened to them (as in Mitchell's untimely death), but to strangers who were not present. The fierce need to talk about death, to reflect on the bitter ironies and nuances of his life, or to even wonder aloud if Mitchell's soul was in transit, were simply avoided.

I was struck by the undercurrent of denial—this ambiguity, if you will—because for decades people have come to me, sometimes in protracted states of terror, to ruminate about these very issues. There is simply no person whose inner life is not haunted by the fear of death or who doesn't grope for comfort with assertions about the afterlife. We live privately in valleys but often gather for these public death rituals only on imaginary high hills.

There was a series of speakers who shared fond anecdotes of the fun-loving, notoriously mischievous Mitchell. Some of the eulogists were sophomoric, cloaking their nervousness about death in their tales of silly pranks and drunken camping expeditions. Others were more dignified, acknowledging the shock and sorrow that Mitchell's wife, ten-year-old son, and parents were suffering. Deep human sympathies were surely conveyed, but the crowd never really heard the story and consequence of Mitchell's life. There was little ruefulness, few expressions of human longings; all but nothing articulated that could be described as heartbreaking, even though this death was particularly heartrending, mysterious, and unresolved. People leaned forward slightly, their lips parted as they listened. But they did not appear to be forming words in their heads. The American way of death does not always invoke gravitas from us. We just have to show up and nod our heads with sympathy.

This was, in the end, a light afternoon romp that mostly avoided any shadows and ultimately evaded the tragic lonesomeness and disbelief that had to have been eating away at Mitchell's family. Nobody even mentioned the word "grief."

A reception followed outdoors along the grassy, seashore garden of the grand lodge. I had performed many weddings at this same spot and the atmosphere and ambience were now similar to this gathering of bereaved friends and family. An army of waiters and attendants labored briskly to supply and service the guests with platters of appetizers, salmon dishes, sushi, beef, salads, and some vegan options. There was a "kids' corner," offering the requisite grilled burgers, hot dogs, french fries, and a selection of ice cream and other desserts.

The servers, clad in smart black-and-white uniforms, handed people shiny plates and silverware and kept the buffet replenished.

Others among the laborers circled the garden and deferentially refilled people's coffee or teacups. And there was a bar set up in one corner that offered wine and spirits. There was much laughter and glibness; people caught up together about their businesses and families.

I noticed that in one corner of the lawn, Susan, the young widow, shy, slim, wearing a chic black dress, was trapped before a line of guests, some of them holding piled plates of food in one hand. They were all anxious to personally offer their condolences—a noble effort, but I could see that it was overwhelming her. She was being prevented from sitting down and having something to eat herself. The memorial service, which included several vivacious and inspiring gospel presentations by a locally renowned, racially mixed choir, had gone on for some two hours. It was now past 1:00 p.m. and people were hungry.

At least twenty individuals, aware they had the chance now to address Susan, successively approached, embraced, and spoke to her. She continuously nodded her head dutifully. She appeared dazed. The sun was high in the sky and the heat added to the widow's gathering weariness. But what also concerned me was that just moments after a ceremony paying tribute to a young father killed in an accident, the ten-year-old son of this widow, Jason, was nowhere near her. I thought the mother and son should be united in this situation, to hearten one another, to serve as a buffer between the well-meaning onslaughts of condolence-givers, and to mourn as wife and child of a man whose life was just remembered.

It was incongruous to me that these two immediate survivors were disconnected from one another at that moment. Maybe I was being self-righteous but that's how I felt. My heart hurt for little Jason in particular. Before the service had begun that morning, he was polite when I approached him to talk but would not engage with me. He smiled at me but then looked down at the floor when I asked him about his dad. It was hard to find his face under his bushy head of blond hair.

Now my eyes scanned the spacious garden lawn and, off in an opposite corner, I saw Jason chewing on a burger in the kids' food sector and not particularly interacting with the other youngsters. I walked over to Susan and, even as people pressed against her, gently took her elbow. "Susan," I said. "You must be hungry. Why don't we find Jason and you two can have a bite together?"

She assented, letting out a breath, and we began to walk in the direction where Jason sat. People still came up to her when they saw her trying to pass by. Finally, we got to Jason. He looked up, unsmiling. She did not lean over nor gather in her son. There was a formality between them, even a distance. I offered to bring her a plate of food and then, after thanking me, she sat down next to her son.

When I returned a few moments later, neither mother nor son was at the table. I saw Jason playing tag with a few other boys nearby, his little blue blazer gone and his shirttail flying. I looked across the lawn area and noticed Susan again standing and surrounded by well-wishers. I felt a sense of failure, and not a little bit bemused by what I thought was strange behavior. It was a mixture of bruised professional pride and a genuine unease about the lost opportunity for the grieving mother and son to begin sustaining each other.

Suddenly, I felt a soft tap my shoulder. Like a feather of memory, it was something perceptible only to me and as undeniable as the situation to which I was ministering at that moment.

I didn't have to turn around or even move at all to discern who was calling on me. It wasn't anybody one could see. It was an old spirit forever alive in my being, intermittently guiding me, correcting me, and cheering me to the realization that in spite of all the chaos and pain in the world, there is an order in the universe that is finally revealed on the other side. Her name on earth was Charlotte Banda and I helped her family to bury her almost twenty years earlier. She didn't whisper to me frequently but I heard her Polish-inflected voice at that moment on the lawn along the Pacific horizon. For me, she remains a talisman from heaven.

"It is not for us to judge. It is for us to help. Honor the mystery, as we have discussed."

Then she was gone. So too was my haughtiness and fervor to manage and fix everything. Bereavement is a book of many chapters. I breathed out in relief and clarity. Charlotte had sent me back to another moment: I remembered my twelve-year-old sister dancing among the headstones nearby while my mother, brother, and I stood over my father's casket being lowered into the ground so long ago. No one interfered or forced my sister to come closer to the open earth and the Hebrew devotions being uttered above the plain pine coffin and the wailing that engulfed the circle. In pure grief, no one was judgmental. We were all doing the best we could in the midst of an unspeakable situation. Grief is personal, idiosyncratic, and age-sensitive. Sometimes it is a dance and sometimes it is a silent retreat. But sooner rather than later, we who suffer it must sit down at its table and eat from its bitterness. That's all we can do as those who are living, hurting, and trying to recover while on this side.

Chapter Two

The Stages of Grief Are Personal: What Do the Dying Teach Us about Life?

· · · · · · · · · · ·

"To live in hearts we leave behind is not to die."
Thomas Campbell

Julie Axelrod, a clinician, has written about the generally understood stages of grief. Like most transitions in human life, the process takes time and it has its own schedule. It is challenging and hard. Dealing with loss is a personal matter; it is as unique as each one of us. Nonetheless, there is widespread agreement on the progression of the stages in bereavement. Axelrod lists the five stages of grief and loss as:

1. **Denial and isolation**. This is the defense and survival mechanism against the emotional shock.

2. **Anger**. We project the anger on others, even blaming others for the death. We discover feelings of anger against the deceased for dying and leaving us alone.

3. **Bargaining**. We are filled with a sense of helplessness mixed in with regrets. ("He wouldn't have died if I/we had done more to help." Therapists and grief counselors generally agree that the bargaining stage (i.e., when we make deals

with the powers above to reverse the painful reality of a death) is especially difficult. "Bargaining is actually a vain expression that the bad news is reversible."[7]

4. **Depression**. We sink into feelings of loss, anguish, and regret. The reality also sets in.

5. **Acceptance**. We finally come to terms with our sorrow and guilt.

People who are grieving do not necessarily go through the stages in the same order or experience all of them.[8]

I believe those in mourning need to move through all the stages before they finally arrive at acceptance. It is not an easy emotional transaction, but it is crucially important. Axelrod's declaration that grieving people do not all experience the exact same steps or not necessarily in perfect order is also significant. Be aware that there are stages, but do not assume you are a textbook case. If you do that, it may cause you deeper confusion and anxiety; you might be asking yourself, "Wait, this is not according to the official cycle. What am I doing or experiencing that is wrong?" When you grieve, you must be yourself. However you pass through, pass through. At some time (and, again, this varies from person to person) you will have progressed to acceptance. There will be a time when you do finally feel that breakthrough. Your beloved dead want you to live.

When I was fourteen years old I witnessed the effect of mortality for the first time, and in public. Being in the direct presence of someone about to depart the earth can help guide us across the bridge of grief. When we prepare for an approaching death or are in recovery, it helps

---

7 Elisabeth Kübler-Ross. *On Death and Dying: What the Dying Have to Teach Doctors, Nurses, Clergy, and Their Own Families.* (New York: Macmillan, New York, 1969).

8 Julie Axelrod, "The Five Stages of Grief and Loss," accessed January 17, 2018, https://psychcentral.com/lib/the-5-stages-of-loss-and-grief.

us to filter our grief with structure and support. My experience has taught me that the more we are exposed to death, the less we will fear it.

The Palmers

Many members of the small congregation to which my family belonged were gathered at a wedding banquet for the children of good friends of my parents. This emotional celebration was filled with hard-working people who shared much joy and sorrow over the years.

Following the marriage ceremony, as people were feting the couple, a hush began to spread through the room. The rabbi of the congregation was coming to pay a visit and he was bringing his wife along. She hadn't been seen much around the community because she was terminally ill with cancer. The arrival of Rabbi Palmer and his wife was of particular interest to us youngsters, who had otherwise been preoccupied with the loud music, the pizza appetizers, and the opposite sex.

As it turned out, the adults in the room knew Rabbi and Mrs. Palmer were coming to say goodbye. They had been with our community for four years and were respected and well liked. Sylvia Palmer, however, wanted to return to her native Australia in order to die there. Many people at that wedding party knew this. The parents of the bride had invited the rabbi and his wife for the whole evening but the Palmers wanted to just stop by and not intrude upon a happy occasion with their anguish.

Rabbi Palmer, a tall tree of melancholy, suddenly appeared on the podium where the band stopped playing. I saw his blue eyes glisten with moisture. He nervously stroked his prematurely gray beard. He was saying something about affection and bonds and milestones that he would now miss, when a ghost appeared from behind him.

Sylvia Palmer was creamy white and drawn. Her smile at first startled us; there seemed to be no breath moving through her mouth and it appeared as though her teeth barely clung to her gums. Her strapping husband held her hand but it looked as though he could have lifted his wife in one palm. Mrs. Palmer wore a wig that was already tipped in the direction of eternity. Some of the people in the room sobbed, but most were spellbound. During what had been a jubilant moment in life, we were all confronted with the reality of mortality. The shadow of grief clung to the hall.

Sylvia Palmer floated toward the microphone. Her husband hovered just behind her, immense yet tender. She stood erect, however, and we saw her eyes still shone with life. Her sad smile came through and she spoke one sentence: "I am grateful for the life I've had and accept what will be."

She then bowed her head slightly in the direction of the mesmerized bride and groom and disappeared behind her aching husband. The space the two visitors had occupied was empty once more. The band played on again, and soon after coffee and dessert were served.

What does this say to you or to any person in mourning? Or to someone who is preparing to lose a loved one? Perhaps we can find an answer given by an eleventh-century scholar named Bahya ben Joseph ibn Pakuda: "Life and death are brothers; they live in the same house. Life is the entrance, death is the exit."[9] Indeed, as we pass through the journey of life, we discern that existence is not unlimited. One by one, our loved ones and friends disappear from view and we become more apprehensive for ourselves.

· · · · · · · · · · ·

When we grieve, we discover that by being human, we are truly vulnerable to cancer, heart disease, any assortment of deficiencies and

9 Kaufmann Kohler and Isaac Broydé, "Bahya ben Joseph ibn Pakuda (also known as Beḥay and Baḥie)" JewishEncyclopedia.com, http://www.jewishencyclopedia.com/articles/2368-bahya-ben-joseph-ibn-pakuda.

viruses, and the aging process. Mortality is the condition we were born with but that went essentially unheeded until the later season of our lives—though people die at all ages. From death, we learn that life ends; from mortality, we learn that life teaches. This is what Charlotte Banda, the soul who signaled me to forbearance at that seaside memorial I described earlier, taught me.

Charlotte, who survived the ghettos, boxcars, and concentration camps of the Nazi Holocaust before arriving in Canada as a teenager, once told me, "Learn from my death. Don't give me all away to it." Charlotte—and your loved one—wanted to be remembered as he or she was *in life*, breathing, coaxing, inspiring, loving, and teaching you and me something of real value. Grief is the direct passageway to their words and deeds and insights.

In short, mortality and the dead themselves implore us to ask: What *is* important?

In the course of my bereavement work, I have observed that a thoughtful acceptance of life's limits can create a personal feeling of well-being. And it can help us deal with the loss of a loved one or a dear friend. A little bit of spirituality can be more helpful than a lot of portfolios; death is oblivious to wealth and holdings, to power and rank.

Death need not be feared and it cannot be evaded in acts of outrage, impropriety, or narcissism. Submit to it just as you participated in life's revelries. Meanwhile, there is often relief in death, tranquility in death, gratitude in death, even blessing in death. Nothing else can happen to your beloved who suffered long and hard in illness and/or without a feeling of dignity and independence. No more pain or humiliation. No more waiting in trepidation. Your dead simply lie or float in utter peace.

I have seen this serenity of acceptance in people who regarded and practiced life with a measure of sanctity and thankfulness. When people die, the way they pass on (unless it is the result of a tragic accident or violence) tends to reflect the way they lived. Folks I knew who were sweet to life generally died sweetly. Those who had something to do with spirituality generally went into "the good night" without a lot of fanfare; those who were hard on themselves and on others struggled proportionately in their deathbeds.

In the course of many years of work with the living and dying, I have learned to regard mortality with respect and reverence, acknowledging its magnificent tyranny as the sure sign that there is some kind of greater hand that guides the universe. And this in turn assures me that there is more to life than our temporary interval on this earth.

Ethan and His Daughters

In *Gates of Repentance: The New Union Prayerbook for the Days of Awe*, a prayer book published by the Central Conference of American Rabbis, it is written:

> If some messenger were to come to us with the offer that death should be overthrown, but with the one inseparable condition that birth should also cease; if the existing generation were given the chance to live forever, but on the clear understanding that never again would there be a child, or a youth, or first love, never again new persons with new hopes, new ideas, new achievements, ourselves for always and never any others—could the answer be in doubt?[10]

I remembered this devotion when visiting with Ethan Forsch, Jr. Ethan was ninety-four years old, in home hospice, dependent upon oxygen, and quite impatient. His two daughters, Betty and Carla, sat on the adjacent bed and kept their teary eyes on their father. "How are things with you, Ethan?" I inquired.

"Rabbi, I am here to die," growled Ethan, a forthright statement uncharacteristic of the death-denying American bereavement culture. Betty and Carla smiled. They knew their father's directness and were grateful for his apparent acceptance of the situation. I thought Ethan's attitude was commendable, as was the acknowledgment of it on the part of his daughters. They all seemed to understand that ninety-four years of life was quite a gift, even in the twenty-first century.

"It's good to hear you declare your readiness to die, Ethan," I responded. "Now we can talk together straight, particularly with your daughters in the room."

"That's fine," barked the old man. He looked tenderly at his two grown children and then spoke to me. "They don't understand how lucky I've been. I lost my one brother when he was nineteen. I don't know why I deserved to live this long. I was doing everything I wanted to until just a few weeks ago. Why do you suppose I'm still around?"

"I guess God isn't too angry with you, Ethan. You have been given long life."

"Oh stop with the theological clichés," scolded Ethan. "Living this long isn't all it's cracked up to be."

"What do you mean?" I was curious and wanted to get some insight from someone who had clearly outlived his own bargain with mortality.

"I mean I did everything I wanted to do and whenever I felt like it. Played golf till just a few months ago. Wow, did I take it all for granted!"

Betty interrupted, "We got him to give up the car just three months ago. He was still driving!"

To this, Carla, visibly filled with warmth for her cantankerous dad, added, "I'm not sure he still wouldn't be behind the wheel of his Buick if he wasn't hooked up to all these things in here."

"Well, whatever," growled her father. "My point is that since I got to live for so long and do what I wanted, why can't I just die already like I want?"

The question hung above the cramped, steam-filled bedroom for a moment. I looked at the two sisters and understood that they supported their father's wish to die sooner rather than later. They were clearly resigned to his end. What we in general often fail to understand is that some people are truly ready to die. Betty and Carla did not seem to maintain any conspiratorial notions about helping their father to a quicker way out of this world. I concluded this was not a question of euthanasia. It was just the matter of a tired man who had had enough of this life and was simply looking forward to leaving it with dignity.

"Ethan," I queried, "how do you wish to be remembered?" The daughters appeared to tense up with the question. The dying man, keenly in touch with his mortality, had set the tone for this encounter. I thought it would be appropriate and supportive for his daughters to hear his testament. Too often, the dying do not take or are not given the opportunity to reveal what they really want said and done at their funeral and beyond.

"How do I want to be remembered? Ethan mused. "Just for having lived for a real purpose," he answered, clearing his throat and taking on a softer tone. Breathing laboriously, he turned toward his daughters, who in turn edged closer to him. "*This* is the purpose," he declared as tears wetted his eyes. He talked to me while he stared at them.

Ethan's hands trembled as he began to do what the dying need to do—he recounted his life and his family history. His grandfather had come from Vienna and peddled goods on the road between Allentown, Pennsylvania, and Toledo, Ohio. Ethan, releasing his soul a bit, remembered many details about his childhood. His father, stern and distracted with making ends meet; his mother, ever-present and dutiful and forever making beds; the beginnings of a prosperous family furniture business; the close-knit neighborhood in Philadelphia; the vagrant uncle who had embarrassed the family with philandering and poor investments; his departed wife, Marisa, who had set such an elegant table at Passover; his comely yet very different daughters.

Betty was like her mother, he said. She was refined and soft-spoken. Carla was shrewd at business and was independent and outspoken. "You were much more like me, sweetie," he told his younger daughter, whose tears showered down to moisten her smile of acceptance. "But it was good, Betty, that one of you was like your mother because she made a man out of me that people could stand being around!"

The grieving process was filling the room because each person was speaking frankly with one another. Ethan chuckled at his own words and we all joined in. Betty and Carla were considerably more at ease now. Their father, though approaching death, was nonetheless himself. Too often, we treat the dying as though they are no longer living, as if the facts of one's mortality suddenly deny him or her those salient characteristics, attributes, or flaws that defined the person. We sometimes forget the very things that made somebody familiar when he or she is dying. And doing that stifles the grieving process; it goes unchanneled or becomes routinized.

If a person sparkled with a sense of humor through life, he wants us to notice and enjoy it all the more at the edge of his mortality—and to be remembered for it. If somebody normally tended to anger, she will likely be angry at the end. When somebody is dying, he or she is the same person, only more so. If he was cantankerous, he will be noticeably cranky while dying. If she was a person of refinement, she will likely appear as sophisticated and courtly as she can. We send that person to an even greater loneliness when we act as though he or she is now altered exactly when that person is trying to define him- or herself for our memory. Being our authentic self with the dying—and letting the dying be his or her authentic self—sets the path for a redemptive grieving process.

I learned a lot from the tenderness and honesty of that moment involving Ethan Forsch, Jr. and his daughters. When he died a few days later, they were aggrieved and in pain, but they were not crippled, because they regarded him in death as the actual person he was in life.

Natalie

"Why can't I live forever?" Natalie demanded of me as I held her hand in the hospital room. This is a question we often hear from those facing the end of life. How we respond is significant and can affect our grief journeys once our loved ones have left this world.

Natalie, sixty-nine at the time, was still relatively youthful, certainly alert and feisty. "Why do I have to die?" she asked. At least she knew her illness had become terminal; her anger confirmed she'd crossed that crucial threshold of acknowledgment. But Natalie was not quite in the mode of acceptance, and my heart went out to her.

She truly enjoyed life and had found expression for this delectation in her classroom. She taught American history to thousands of high school students for more than forty years. "I miss those kids," she lamented. *Those kids.* She held the phrase on her lips as though reluctant to let loose of it. Natalie Rothschild and her husband, Fred, who had died suddenly several years before, had two adult sons. One was a state tourism official and the other taught English in Morocco. But *those kids*—her pupils—were the ones Natalie craved now, in her hospital room, where she was being treated for a losing battle with lupus, an unyielding disease.

"The wolves are coming to get me," she said one day, bitterly denouncing the association of the carnivorous *Canis lupus* with her disease. "Look at my face and you'll see where they have left their marks." There were, in fact, noticeable lesions on Natalie's cheeks as well as along her fingertips. The skin along her fingernails was thin and flaky from the malady, which is rarely fatal. Natalie was unlucky; a pervasive rash attacked the flesh around her nose. She was dying.

Medication and treatment had helped her intermittently over the years. It was clear that what gave Natalie the ability to overcome fatigue, joint pain, and afflicted blood serum was her great will. Poise in life breeds dignity in death. And it teaches us, the survivors, to be dignified and focused as we work through our sorrow.

Natalie would settle back in her bed, breathe out from pain, and tell me again about Ethan Allen, the Revolutionary War general. "You know," she'd repeat, "they would come and tell him, when he was sick, that the angels were waiting for him. And do you know what he said? He said, 'They're waiting, eh? Well, God damn them, let them wait!'" And again, the hoarse bitter laugh would emerge from the tall but failing woman, shaking the bed frame.

I asked Natalie, "What about your sons? Do they come to see you?"

Her face turned dark. "They haven't come around too often. Granted, the one is in Morocco. But they don't seem to be in contact."

"What did you talk about with your sons when they were here?" I asked.

"Oh, their careers, their houses, their friends. I think the weather came up and there was a reference or two to NBA basketball." *What an alert, intuitive—if indignant—woman is this Natalie*, I thought.

"What did you want them to talk about?"

"Well, maybe something about their mother, for God's sake. I am dying here."

"I understand."

Natalie looked at me impatiently. She did not speak, and just closed her eyes. She folded her arms across her chest; I noticed the rash build-up on her palms. Clearly, her sons' visits had been inconclusive, perhaps painful. Members of a family were not being honest with each other about their mortality. I felt sad for Natalie, her sons, her three rarely mentioned grandchildren, and her departed husband. There might have been an opportunity for closure, forgiveness, or insight squandered here. As I ruminated, Natalie suddenly opened her eyes and burst out laughing.

"What?" I asked, startled and relieved.

"My son, Jerry, the one who lives in Morocco, remembered something while he was here that my husband once did. Fred took the boys, Jerry and Todd, to Canada one summer. The boys were in high school. I was teaching a summer school course. Fred wanted to show them Canada just in case they'd eventually have to go up there to avoid the draft. It was during Vietnam. Fred hated that war and wouldn't tolerate his sons fighting in such a conflict. Well, anyway, he took them up there to go fishing but he also wanted some of those damned Cuban cigars."

Natalie paused, smiling a bit, while wiping away a tear. "You know, he was such an idiot! He takes his sons up to Canada so they can learn about avoiding a war against Communists in Asia, but he also sneaks back into the United States with a package of Cuban cigars." She looked at me for some indication of my reaction.

"It sounds like he knew what he believed in and what he wanted to smoke."

The teacher chuckled and then stared at me. "It's a good thing you never took one of my classes, Rabbi. I don't like canned answers." She continued reliving the moment, now quite animated, as her memories of Fred's broad personality and the aroma of burning cigars drifted into the septic hospital room. "Anyway, as they approach the border at Fort Erie—you know, across from Buffalo—the boys remind him that the Cuban cigars are illegal. They tell him he'd better think of something because they're going to be asked what they bought by the guard at the border. Todd, the funny one, tells Fred that if he's ever going to run away to Canada to avoid serving in Vietnam, he doesn't want to have a cigar felony on his record already!"

Natalie took a long breath, drawing comfort from the recollections of her loved ones. Similarly, we who survive the death of a dear person keep his soul afloat by remembering him faithfully as he was. Natalie continued, "God, he was silly, that Fred of mine. I'm sorry you never knew him. We had a great time. My kids at school used to ask me why I always had so much energy. My classroom was a wonderful place. I told them, each time, that I had energy because my life has a purpose. Go find your purpose, I'd say." Now Natalie stopped, and the tears came. Tears bittersweet with her mortality. She collected herself and said, "But you know what? My purpose . . . was life with Fred."

Natalie put her head in her scarred hands and began to cry and heave. I put one hand on hers as her tears dripped down her cheeks. After a few moments passed, I passed a cup of water to her and she sipped it with a straw. No words passed between us for this interlude; none were necessary. Finally, more composed, she spoke again, even offering a faint smile.

"So meanwhile, Fred has got those cigars in the car that he can't imagine parting with. Isn't it strange? I can tell you about the entire history of the United States, but I'm stuck on my husband and his Cuban cigars."

"So what happened?"

"Ha! Thank you for not putting on airs like some of the doctors and a few visitors. Look, I know I am really sick. I know I'm so damn unlucky because lupus doesn't usually kill people. I'm not stupid. I know my situation. People come in here and act like they're talking to a dead person. But I'm still alive! While I'm still here, I wish people would not whisper in my presence like I'm some kind of defunct cow."

"I understand, Natalie."

"So tell me then, Rabbi, why me? Why is this happening to me?"

"I'm not going to patronize you with some kind of rabbinic passage or a cliché, Natalie. I don't know why it's happening to you. But what I do know is that I want to do my part in helping you leave this world with a measure of peace."

A long silence. Natalie closed her eyes for a few moments and then opened them.

"So," I asked after a decent interval. "What happened with the cigars?"

"Oh, God. The cigars. Well, Fred decides to put them in a brown bag and hide them in a place where the customs official wouldn't look. He pulls over and tucks them somewhere in the engine. Jerk!" Natalie was giggling now. "The customs guy comes over and starts talking to Fred and the boys. Where have you been? What did you buy? Suddenly the air outside is filling with the definite aroma of cigars. Fred tries to look innocent and the customs guy can only chuckle. The motor is smoking Fred's illicit Cubans!"

Natalie was now laughing with relief and affection. "Finally, the officer leans into Fred's window and says, 'Sir, I hope they were illegal so I can feel good about the confiscation.' They were allowed to pass. The car smelled like Havanas for days. I didn't let Fred off the hook about that one for a long time!"

Natalie Rothschild died a couple of days later. In a final conversation, I asked her if she wanted to pray with me. She scoffed at the idea, saying, "That's not for me. I taught history. Everybody I taught about is gone. It's my turn to make some room. I just hope some of those kids heard me."

We mourners went to the cemetery and buried Natalie next to Fred. Their two sons, now totally orphaned, said very little and remained stiff and formal. I was concerned they would not know how to properly grieve because their relationship with their mother had been so starched. I might have known more about the inner life of Natalie Rothschild than they did. We have to be present in someone's life in order to fully deal with his or her death.

Nonetheless, the buckeyes swayed in the autumn wind. It was a bit too early for the snows. When we walked away, I thought I smelled a wisp of cigar smoke and could have sworn I heard some familiar laughter.

Chapter Three

Honoring a Loved One: What to Do, What to Say at a Time of Grief

· · · · · · · · · · ·

"Can I see another's woe,
And not be in sorrow too?
Can I see another's grief,
And not seek for kind relief?"
William Blake

So often people have called me and asked, "Rabbi, my father [or someone else] has died. What do I do now?"

This is exactly what a friend of mine, Hayley, asked just hours after her father succumbed to old age and a series of maladies. Like many of us these days, Hayley, a woman in her fifties, was also dealing with the geographic issues associated with living, caretaking, and the death of a loved one from far away. Although she had made frequent trips across the country during her father's final months—Hayley lives in Southern California and her dad finished his life in Binghamton, New York—the realities were exacerbated by the distance. But it is always hard, even if all the parties are in the same physical place.

"I Want to Die at Home."

If someone dies at home, it can be both a blessing and a challenge. The blessing is in the close proximity of loved ones. This is obviously not always feasible and is sometimes simply a matter of circumstance. No one should feel shame or guilt if he or she were simply unable to be at the bedside when someone drew his or her last breath. But it is good—and therapeutic—if you can attend to the dying as much as possible in their final days. Significant conversations take place, forgiving moments, and even the opportunity to say goodbye is beneficial for both the dying and their loved ones. Closure requires closing interludes. There are remarkable, cleansing exchanges of healing honesty, treasured remembrances, and, in some cases, shared prayer. The dying want to be a part of the conversation as much as possible. Like the earlier-mentioned Ethan Forsch, Jr. and Natalie Rothschild, they wish to be heard. Like Charlotte Banda, they want to be sure they will be remembered. The dying frequently want us to listen to their sensibilities and directives regarding their own funeral. And, generally, few people want to die alone.

I almost always hear an especially expressed relief and thankfulness when a family member tells me, "We were all there with her. It was very peaceful." This is a fortuitous situation (not always attainable) but survivors are encouraged to be present, if at all manageable. With modern medicine it is possible to have a general idea when someone who has been terminally ill will expire. It is a bittersweet, hands-on conclusion that gives us a unique insight as we begin the trek across the bridge of grief. There is nothing quite like feeling the departure of a human soul. Many people have told me that it can *actually* be felt. The profound quietude of this departure envelops and softens the inescapable anguish and sorrow that floods the room when we see someone leave this earth. It doesn't just happen at home. This kind of tender passage is also possible if the death occurs in a hospital, retirement home, or hospice environment. It is more about who is there than where it occurs.

The difficult issue in a home death has to do more with practicalities. Sooner rather than later, the body has to be removed. Certainly, an interlude with the deceased is necessary. There is no set or "correct" protocol that comes with this pause. Some people need to wail, others to touch and kiss their beloved, and still others must utter some further departing words in the direction of the body. This is a moment unlike any other in our lives. We are, at once, bearing feelings of helplessness, inspiration, confession, abandonment, relief, and frightfulness. All this is mixed with devotion and longing and a searing awareness of our own mortality. If so moved, someone may wish to close the eyes of the deceased. It is not necessary to immediately cover his or her face under the blanket or sheet, unless people are uncomfortable otherwise.

This moment is a milestone of incalculable proportions and will be retained in your heart and mind with uncompromising clarity. It imprints your soul.

Nevertheless, action is required. There have been times I was with a family at home when their beloved died. They needed other professionals besides me at that point. In many cases, the family had established a relationship with a funeral home. Perhaps the now-deceased and family members had made arrangements in advance—an extremely prudent idea. In the American funeral industry, this is called "pre-needs," and it spares the survivors a great deal of indecision and unnecessary costs at such a moment. The family has had the memorial preplanned with direct input from their beloved one. They do not have to second-guess what he or she wanted to have done, what kind of casket to choose, where exactly will be the burial spot, who will speak, and what will be the religious component, if any. It was all declared and contracted, even years prior, by the person now being mourned.

Without these earlier provisions, people are forced to make painful decisions under great duress—an almost certain avenue to in-family disputes and conflicts. Of course, it is not always possible for someone to make his or her arrangements in advance. Some people are reluctant to do so and some people die suddenly or just don't live long enough to really think about it. When someone dies, we work with what we have. But, candidly, the mortuaries, cemeteries, and cremation societies are in business. They generally charge a lot more for their services if there isn't a pre-needs contract and the freshly grieving are considerably more susceptible to their financial demands than they would have been in a calm, reflective atmosphere long before this terrible day.

Either way, a mortuary needs to be phoned within an hour or so of a person's death at home. If hospice workers are present, they make all the calls and arrangements. If not, and no one has the number of a mortuary, then 911 can be dialed. A team will arrive and properly retrieve the body. Someone over eighteen years of age must complete a Pronouncement of Death form. The date and time on the form will become the official time of death. One has to be prepared for the fact that this whole process in the house takes awhile. A police officer may sometimes be present to ascertain that the death was natural and does not require an investigation.[11]

If the death occurs in a hospital, the law generally requires the person completing the Pronouncement of Death form to notify the hospital's organ procurement staff. That staff will then talk with the family about the opportunity to donate organs or tissue. Obviously, it's easier to know the answers if the decedent left behind a directive in writing or on a driver's license.

In many cases, there are religious rituals that must be honored (wrapping the body in cotton or linen sheets, for example, if this is a Jewish or Islamic situation). This is out of respect and to prevent the leakage of body fluids during transport. However, the civil paperwork serves as the official Death Certificate that is pending. Regardless of the circumstances, the county coroner has technical requirements that must be followed. Depending upon the way a person died, the removal

11 These procedures will be detailed extensively in Chapter Six, in which two funeral directors are interviewed and describe what they and their staff do.

team has to undertake biohazard checks and controls. If there are any suspicious, traumatic, or ambiguous elements to the death, the body will first be turned over to the coroner's officer for an examination and autopsy. In all cases, a death registration form must be filed with the county. Again, the living are confronted by the bureaucracy of mortality. It can be agonizing for a family still numb from the shock of death. But no life insurance company, for example, will release funds to beneficiaries without an official Death Certificate. In short, there are a lot of necessary strangers involved in handling that most precious of things—the body of a dear deceased.

But not so for the soul. I believe a loved one's soul is known only to those closest to the deceased and resists all functional intruders. I've been around death for too long not to sense and *know* this. When I watch people say goodbye to someone, or tenderly place a religious shawl or symbol on or around them; when I witness them affectionately arrange special objects, jewelry, photos, or letters in the casket; when they lean over and kiss their loved one, I actually feel the flow and cycle of human life emanating from the scene. It has made me believe, unequivocally, that there is something greater than what I see in this universe of humankind.

I have spent many years studying and writing about the life and work of Dr. Martin Luther King Jr. I've been told by someone who was present when the intimate and grieving colleagues of Dr. King came to see his body at St. Joseph Hospital just after his assassination in Memphis on April 4, 1968, they comforted each other by saying, "That's not all of him."[12]

The body is simply the temporary housing, the interim shell of the spirit. When the spirit is freed by physical death then the body has completed its purpose in this world. But the soul has an eternity

12 Corroborated for me in 2010 personally by Rev. Samuel "Billy" Kyles of Memphis, TN.

that transcends both theology and science. It is the ladder that links heaven and earth. How is this process initiated? By simply *remembering* someone you give his soul wings; you can practically hear her voice, see his face, recall the shape of her hands. Memory leavens grief and allows the soul of a loved one to live close to you. It's only when no one remembers someone any longer that the person dies. So, ultimately, it doesn't matter how people are transported away from us. What matters is how they stay with us.

Listening with Love

Meanwhile, how does one talk to the grieving? Let's start with this idea: less is more. It is often difficult to simply listen; you may feel uneasy and want to fill an awkward gap with chatter. But listening can offer solace to those in sorrow. They need to express themselves, and too much talk or clichés can cramp their ability to do so—it can even backfire.

"I'm sorry your father passed." I heard a visitor use this common expression with a mournful son during a condolence call. It was well intended and genuine, but it lacked the desired effect. Certain words sometimes come off as banal and trigger a negative reaction.

Moments later, with the earnest visitor out of earshot, the mourner said to me, "What did my father pass? The bar exam? His driver's license test? My father's dead. The fellow could have just said he's sorry my father died. He's having a harder time talking about my father than I am."

There are many ways to talk about someone's death or to emotionally reference our overriding mortality. Most people truly do the best they can. But when somebody else dies, it's almost guaranteed that we will think of our own inevitable death. Phrases such as "passed away," "no longer with us," "been called to God," and the like transmit a message that cloaks our own apprehensions.

These are gentle euphemisms for the hard truth and they can blur the therapy of grief. They are not harmful or sinful, but they do occasionally sound like rationalizations. We Americans are usually straightforward and do not use metaphors, about, say, our bank accounts. Yet we are strangely solicitous about our mortality. The latter is more certain and has a firmer bottom line than the former.

Sheryl Sandberg, the Facebook COO, lost her forty-seven-year-old husband David Goldberg suddenly in 2015. She has published and spoken extensively about her excruciating journey in the aftermath. In 2017, she wrote about the challenge of dialogue during fresh mourning:

> You have to find ways to break the isolation. I found it very hard to tell people that I wanted to talk. It felt like I was imposing my sadness on them. When someone asked, "How are you?" I kept saying, "I'm fine," and then people wouldn't ask me any questions. But I learned to say, "I'm actually not doing that well." One of the most common things about grief, about loss, about adversity, is silence. So what happen is, you go through this adversity or trauma, and then what piles on top of that is the isolation of no one talking about it.[13]

When talking about death, we are talking about one of the sure things in life. We should be compassionate, judicious with our words, caring—but not equivocal. We should not dance around the topic. We should be gentle but not indirect, even if the customs of language seem to obscure the realities. Regardless of whatever afterlife may or may not exist, the fact is someone is gone from this world and that person will never be seen again in the flesh. When attending to a family at the time of a funeral, I don't impose a lot of practices, because I think people all grieve differently. Yet one thing I do require is that the survivors see the casket lowered into the ground. I invite them to use a shovel or their own hands to throw some dirt onto the lowered container. The thud of the earth on the box is shattering but it conveys finality. Understanding

13 "Healing Advice: Sandberg's Hard-Won Wisdom on How to Recover," published in *AARP: The Magazine,* June/July 2017, p. 51.

the finality of the situation, in words, rituals, and actions is painful, but it is all critical for each one of us to grasp it as we grasp onto the bridge of grief and the healing on the other side.

Norman

I was faced with a real communication challenge years ago. Norman Blake, a bright but forlorn musician in his forties, killed himself in Los Angeles. Even before this tragedy, his aged parents hardly ever left their apartment in Cleveland because they had never quite recovered from their daughter Frederica's suicide several years prior. There was some sort of spiritual dysfunction in this ill-fated family. Two out of their three children ended their lives deliberately. How was I going to tell the Blakes that Norman had replicated Frederica's awful act?

I received word about Norman from his other sister, Marla, who also lived on the West Coast. Brave, suffering, yet somehow unstopped by this development, Marla expressed one overriding concern to me on the telephone. "Rabbi, you've got to go tell my parents. I can't do it over the phone. Please go let them know and I'll be home tomorrow."

I contacted a few members of the extended family in town; they all knew and were paralyzed with sorrow and uncertain how to approach Norman's parents. We had to work and coordinate quickly. I worked up enough courage to drive over to the apartment house. Several relatives would wait in the lobby until I rang down to them. I had called Mr. Blake before coming over and told him I wanted to stop by for a visit. "Fine, Rabbi," he said, sounding resigned to something. Later, the bereaved father would tell me that he suspected a solicitation from me on behalf of our synagogue.

I walked in and sat down. The couple, gray and already weary from life, politely asked me the reason for my appointment. I opened my mouth and told them.

"It's about Norman. I'm afraid Norman is dead."

"What?" The two parents recoiled in horror. I kneeled on the carpet near them and held out both arms in support to each of them.

Mrs. Blake's eyes rolled in shock. "Norman? Dead? Was it an accident?"

Mr. Blake seemed to discern what was coming. I said, "No it wasn't an accident. I'm sorry to say that Norman took his own life. It happened in his apartment in Los Angeles. Marla called me. She's fine. She's flying home right now. I'm so sorry to come over and share such news. You don't deserve this. But Norman is dead."

"Normy!"

The mother's shriek filled the tiny room. Mr. Blake, in a stony state, nodded at me. He understood. He had been there before. His suffering was palpable.

Meanwhile, the mother was inconsolable. "I understand that Freddie had to do it. But Normy? Why, Normy, why?" She rocked in pain, falling into her husband's limp arms. I held onto them a little longer, and then drew back. I was certain they comprehended. I went over to the telephone and called down to the lobby. Soon the apartment was filled with family members.

People tried to comfort one another. Slowly, plans were made as the hideous reality settled in. I eventually withdrew from the scene and went out to sit in my car. I struggled to put the key into the ignition slot and realized that my hands were trembling. I felt my throat tightening. I saw Norman's departed sister, Frederica, lying in her coffin just a few short years earlier. I gasped for some air, wiping tears from my eyes. I drove off, satisfied that I had told the Blakes exactly what they had to hear.

"I Don't Know What to Say."

So how does one talk to the dying? I have been asked this an incalculable number of times; it is a natural question that arises from the most authentic of concerns. I always emphasize the first thing to do when visiting a terminally ill person—be it at home, in hospice, or in any setting—is to remember that a person who is dying is still a person who is living. This person wants you to be yourself just as he or she remains him- or herself, physical condition notwithstanding. Of course, this may not be applicable in cases of dementia or other debilitating situations. Those visiting are certainly encumbered when they attempt to comfort or just listen to someone who, in one way or another, is "not there." However, it is clear to me—and scientific evidence corroborates this—that even those in a coma may very well be aware of our presence and do absorb our words, as well as a gentle touch on their hands or forehead.

The renowned Dr. Elisabeth Kübler-Ross, the pioneer of death and dying research, once affirmed, "I say to people who care for people who are dying, if you really love that person and want to help them, be with them when their end comes close. Sit with them—you don't even have to talk. You don't have to do anything but really be there with them."[14]

When you visit someone at the end of his life, do not, if at all possible, stand or loom above him. Take a seated position level with and close to your loved one. Again, it is always good to physically reach out to him. Perhaps if it is a family member, or just someone very dear to you, offer a kiss on the forehead. In the course of the visit, extend or lay down your hand on one of his hands from time to time. Your instincts will guide you. No tactile contact at all might make the person feel contaminated or undesirable. Offer the first words.

"How are you feeling today?" is not necessarily the best thing to ask up front. And it also is not the finest idea to lunge forward verbally with such cants as "I know you are going to be all right," or "Keep your spirits up." Such clichés rarely help or are simply unconvincing, and they reveal

14 Eliot Jay Rosen, *Experiencing the Soul: Before Birth, During Life, after Death* (Carlsbad: Hay House, Inc. 1998).

your own insecurities or apprehensions about being with a person who is going to die soon.

What I say to someone soon to die is simply, "I've been thinking a lot about you." That's my opening. There's no real need to offer anything else, certainly nothing formulaic. This tends to acknowledge the situation and frees the moment from much of the painful uneasiness. You're not starting with pity. The person *knows* you feel badly for him or her. You are entering with empathy and you are not telegraphing your own fears. That person has enough of his or her own at this edge of eternity and doesn't need to add the burden of yours.

This encounter is about the individual, not the setting. More often than not, if the person is still communicative, he or she will respond to "I've been thinking a lot about you" with some kind of statement, lament, or even just a sigh. It opens the way to a conversation that he or she is leading. Follow the individual's lead even though you may not have a specific reply to some statements or questions.

You might be asked, "Why me? Why is this happening to me?" You probably don't have an answer to this question and shouldn't pretend that you do. A sympathetic nod might be sufficient; you are helping the person by simply acknowledging the anguished query. When I sensed an individual truly wanted some explanation, I have often replied, "I don't know," and spoken their name. "I don't know, Dan. But what I do know is that I care deeply about you and want to spend time with you."

If the person is in any way spiritual or is turning back to his faith now, it can be helpful to quietly suggest, "It might just be that God thinks you are special." This statement can actually be comforting to the dying. They are really afraid and your suggestion that God is specifically interested in their plight is not disingenuous. It can be a balm for their terrifying loneliness. But, again, choose your words sparingly. Remember that whenever you are clearly listening, you are definitively not saying the wrong thing.

Don't make the mistake I once made years ago when I was a much less experienced rabbi. A relatively young woman in my congregation at the time had been diagnosed with an aggressive cancer. She was married to one of the synagogue lay leaders and they made an appealing, energetic, and very philanthropic couple. Everyone loved Lynn and was aggrieved about her ominous diagnosis at the age of forty-two.

During a visit with her in the hospital, Lynn asked me what I thought of her prospects. Eager to promote optimism, I answered, "You know, I believe you will be okay." (Once again, the American tendency toward reflexive cheerfulness—even in mortality situations—prevailed.) Lynn smiled faintly, but I sensed she wasn't convinced.

Two weeks later, I saw her again. She sat up in her hospital bed and her face was filled with shadows and apprehension. But she was also angry . . . at me. "Rabbi, you shouldn't have told me that I'd be okay when you really did not know. The doctors have given me a terminal diagnosis. I have only a few weeks to live. That was irresponsible of you. Don't go around giving people false hope."

She was so right and I was completely devastated and ashamed. In spite of her disappointment in me, she forgave me and allowed that my intentions had been good. But my heedless behavior had done her no good. Since then, I honor Lynn's memory by remaining circumspect and judicious in every situation involving either the dying or the grieving.

So yes, the dying ask questions. They ask, "How could God do this to me?" "How will my family carry on without me?" These heartrending inquiries are certainly difficult to hear. We provide part of the answer each time by just being present for them in their anguished state. They are so often terrified of the abyss. When they verbalize to us, "I am afraid," we need to acknowledge their fears. Maybe we can respond with "I understand." Maybe it's as simple as taking their hand and letting them feel the kindness and devotion we hold in our heart. Maybe that tenderness gives them the response they need and deserve.

Those at the end of life frequently have asked me, "Will I be reunited with my husband (or another family member who is already deceased)?" It is fully appropriate in such an instance to reply, "Yes." I do not believe this to be disingenuous. It is reassuring and supportive. There is no risk involved. The fact is that it is entirely possible that we human beings are rejoined with our beloved in whatever the next dimension is. This kind of message to the dying does not mislead them. Rather, it helps to *lead* them across the bridge. A reunion in heaven is what we all hope for anyway.

In the end, the beacon standard in the challenging and sacred intervals we spend with the dying and the grieving is *being yourself.* The people we are attending to are certainly being themselves in their grueling predicaments. Say little but do much simply by being present. Listen, listen, listen. They want to be heard and, to whatever extent possible, they don't want to be alone.

Chapter Four

How Grief Can Complicate One's Life: What Should I Do in the Days after the Funeral?

· · · · · · · · · · ·

*"When you are born, you cry, and the world rejoices.
When you die, you rejoice, and the world cries."*
Buddhist saying

There is some social awkwardness and spiritual confusion in the moments and days right after a memorial service of any kind. There is the release of initial closure that the ceremony hopefully creates. Depending upon the circumstances of the death, some people actually experience various levels of relief. This is, of course, much more likely if the departed was older and/or suffered a long and debilitating illness. It is normal to have such feelings of reprieve when a loved one is finally suffering no more.

However, there is rarely a sensation of relief when a child or a younger adult dies, or a dear one succumbs to a drug overdose, or is killed in an automobile accident, or commits suicide, or is murdered. How a person leaves this earth has a direct impact upon how one grieves—emotionally, spiritually, and physically. Every demise is a singular moment and, therefore, all the regimented formalities of the faiths do not necessarily work or alleviate the agony. There is no absolute standard in this just as there is no definitive formula about how to experience life. Death is as personal as the person who dies.

I don't reject the mourning practices of my faith, but I also never start to legislate doctrine when people are freshly bereaved. They need to be served at their point of need. They should never be made to feel guilty because they are not familiar with or don't follow this or that timeworn ritual. Their hearts are broken; I can teach them theology another day. Nobody should be judging; we should be remembering.

People have asked me: Should I just stay home and weep for a few days? When should I return to work? When can I go out to the movies or to a restaurant with friends? How many days away from everything familiar and routine is acceptable?

Some of the organized faiths' offerings and practices do provide structure and guidance and a dogmatic order that often soothes and reassures bereaved people suffering through the chaos of loss. People who don't observe a faith should not disparage anyone who truly requires the codes and liturgies of regulated traditions in order to cope with fresh grief. Whatever we are doing or not doing to manage the sorrow, we are all crossing the same bridge of mortality.

I've noticed that Protestant Christianity normally doesn't impose a preset amount of time for the fixed period of formal mourning. In the Christian community, family and friends linger with the dead; there are often wakes, also called visitations, held at home or in a church or in a funeral parlor. This is generally known as the Vigil Service among Catholics. The body is present, the casket is open; people gather around, reminiscing, eating, and personally paying respects. This rite—basically informal and preceding the official church service—is unknown in the Jewish and Islamic communities. Jews and Muslims do not linger with their dead; they bury as soon as possible, within a day—particularly the Muslims. However, the widely assumed twenty-four-hour deadline for burial among the Jews is rarely enforced in America except among the fundamental or Orthodox sects.

Hindus strive to hold the cremation service before the sun goes down on the same day that death takes place. Buddhists, who also usually cremate their dead, spend six days in reflection. The virtuous attributes of the deceased are quietly commemorated, pointing the soul in the direction of eternal life with the Buddha. The memorial ceremony, conducted unpretentiously by a monk, occurs on the seventh day in an atmosphere of marked dignity and modesty.

Jews and Muslims eschew embalming and autopsies. However, there are instances when the coroner, for legal considerations, commands an autopsy even if the family protests due to religious sensibilities. Ironically, the Hebrew Bible specifically records that Joseph was embalmed in Egypt before his body was transported to the Promised Land. So a lot of these faith-driven customs and traditions have evolved and are not consistent with scriptural texts. Clerics have simply invented them.

I don't impose interment within twenty-four hours in my faith tradition because I believe we must be both reasonable and pragmatic. Very few extended families all live in the same locality anymore. People require time to travel from other states or provinces or even other countries. After all, what's more important: that the funeral take place according to what's in some old tomes written by certain members of a long-abandoned demographic, or that people be allowed to arrive and support the immediate family? Give folks an extra day or two to form a circle of comfort.

Since a Christian funeral is usually held within a week after a person has died, the period of time from death to burial is established *de facto* as the time of mourning. Most will return to work as soon as this bereavement period has ended. Jews have a post-funeral interval known as *shiva*, which actually means "seven." But rarely do American Jews

remain at home and out of circulation for a full seven days; it now tends
to be two to three days. Muslims maintain a firmer pattern of three days
of bereavement and devotions at home, with visitors offering sustenance
and care. For Muslim widows, the period is extended to four days, and
they are forbidden to interact with men during this time lest the man be
a potential new suitor.

Now What?

No religious doctrine can be proven wiser than any other, and the only
established and universal fact is that people die and survivors grieve.
It's also easy to notice a pattern of similarities among the several faith
traditions mentioned here when it comes to bereavement. Suffering,
souls, survival, and sanctity all pervade the human condition. President
John F. Kennedy, speaking just five months before his tragic death,
declared, "For, in the final analysis, our most basic common link is
that we all inhabit this small planet. We all breathe the same air. We all
cherish our children's futures. And we are all mortal."[15]

Death is the common denominator of life. So what are our best
options for beneficial behavior and good recovery when we become the
grieving? Perhaps the most repeated and most conclusive question that
people ask after the loss of a loved one is "Should I just stay home and
weep for several days?" In other words, *what do I do*?

You certainly should consider whether to jump immediately into
the normal pattern of things. This probably will not avail you. Don't go
to the movies the day after the funeral or back to work because you are
determined to establish that "everything will be normal. That is what he
wanted." I believe the dead want to be commemorated and remembered
in the manner in which they lived. If someone was fairly religious,
it's good to honor his memory with some rituals. If someone did not

15 John F. Kennedy Commencement Address at American University, Washington,
DC, June 10, 1963.

particularly practice a faith, there is no context to suddenly become observant—unless you yourself happen to be devout. How *the departed* lived is your guide to how he or she should be remembered. But the key is not to rush through the process, regardless of how the process takes shape.

Don't try to be stoic; it only stifles recovery. Let people take care of you. Allow others to worry about the coffee and the food platters and the arriving flowers. Let go; this is a tender transition. You need to sob and then you need to be angry with the person who left (which is perfectly normal), and then you need to declare out loud how much you miss him or her. There are well-documented stages in grief elucidated by a number of intuitive and learned authorities on death and bereavement, such as the aforementioned Elisabeth Kübler-Ross, David Kessler, and others.

You need to rest your broken heart and heal it with the compassion, wisdom, and sustenance of family and friends. I have already stressed how important it is to lean into your grief and to be aware of the emotional and psychological dangers lurking if you sidestep the pain. It's not about how long you stay home; it's about *how* you stay home. Home is the safest sanctuary in the world. As a high school teacher taught me decades ago, "home" is the most beautiful word in any language. It's the safest place to be, particularly at a time of sorrow.

Grief knows no clock and it surely does not comply with a business schedule. At home, you can cry when you want, shriek when you need to, wear what you wish, and, if you are inclined, pray in any fashion that soothes your soul—with or without prepared text or lyrics. However many days you stay at home, whether it's two days or seven, you are protecting your raw psyche from a frenetic world that demands your accession to program and data and bosses and noise and the banalities that simply drain you exactly at the time you are feeling empty.

The conversations, the caresses, the shared memories, and the informative silences that take place at home with loved ones and close friends are often therapeutic and enriching. Take a moment to chuckle about the sometimes funny and familiar traits and habits of the person who has died. There is great release and recuperation in these bursts of laughter. In this sheltering environment, you slowly adjust to the new reality even as your moods shift and your soul is alternately flustered and calmed.

. . . .

We learn a lot about our friends during this time of bereavement. Most of them arrive selflessly, without fanfare, and with the pure intention of serving our needs. They are present and earnest and empathetic. They open the doors for other visitors, pour the coffee, arrange the platters, and clean up the scattered cups and dishes. More importantly, they bear our laments and dry our tears.

And then there are others who strangely vanish from sight or don't even call at this bittersweet threshold of friendship. "I can't go over there now," some people will say. "It's too upsetting. I can't deal with it." Some grievers have told me in the aftermath, "I found out who my friends *really* are. Some people really surprised me by being there. Others really surprised me by never showing up or even calling or dropping a line."

Many people don't "go over there" because they dread the environment of a household in mourning. They can't know or imagine the pain that is sometimes caused by their absence. It is a worthwhile experience to visit and thus show respect. One generally grows and gains insight and satisfaction through such a sojourn. Jews regard it as a *mitzvah*—a good deed. Christians see it as a showing of mercy. It is an act of charity and revelation that soothes the heart of both the giver and receiver. It can help you make peace with your own mortality.

After the Funeral

I recall two exchanges that occurred during the *shiva* at home following my father's sudden death in 1976. One was terribly distracting, the other remarkably considerate and uplifting.

My father died while playing handball at the local community center—in spite of being warned by doctors to avoid the strenuous sport. He had suffered a mild heart attack three years prior. Nonetheless, given that he appeared vital and robust at forty-five years old, there was considerable shock and disbelief at his death among his family and friends.

Our house filled up with visitors after the burial, which took place hurriedly and within twenty-four hours of the fatal heart attack. Most of the guests were truly shaken, solicitous, attentive, and helpful to my devastated mother and us three children. Not a lot of talking went on; the long interludes of silence in the crowded living room said everything.

On the second or third day, a gentleman appeared whom we knew only marginally. I doubted that he actually knew my father personally; some people seem to regularly appear at houses of mourning—for the food, maybe, or out of curiosity. This man's connections to our family were dubious. The only commonality was that he also frequented the Jewish Community Center where my dad had died. He entered and sat down during a lull in the throng of visitors across from where my mother, brother, sister, and I sat on hard mourner's chairs (a practice in Orthodox Judaism). Our torn black ribbons were pinned to our clothing and our hearts lay broken beneath that clothing.

"So," the man asked presumptuously, "what actually happened to your dad?"

None of us could or wanted to answer. The unwelcome guest was sending us right back to the beginning of our bewilderment over my father's death. His inquiry was selfish, inappropriate, and unsettling. I eventually attempted to answer politely, "He had a heart attack at the Jewish Center." I formed the words in my mouth but they did not emerge. It was too surreal a moment. I could not distinguish between the fresh pain that resulted from the question and my indignation that it was even asked. Fortunately, for this tiresome man and us, another visitor deftly and discreetly whisked him out the front door, replete with a little plate of pastry and fruit.

The next night, it was warm and muggy in our house. The general shock had begun to give way to a watery, aching realization that this was not a bad dream. Sometimes, the hardest days are a few days after the death as the initial numbness begins to disintegrate. The funeral, the tributes, the gatherings, and the outpourings yield to the comprehension that somebody's place is empty and that he or she is simply not coming back.

Despite the heat, the house again filled with people. Soon a small group of my classmates from the local rabbinical school entered. I looked up gratefully at my friend Peter. Peter was a tall, lanky man who prayed hard and played the banjo. He hailed from Texas, and once strummed for a Jewish cowboy rock band. He stood before me as I sat weeping on the mourner's stool. Peter did not say a word. He took his bare hand and, with a motion as gentle as that of an angel, wiped the sweat off my brow and the tears off my cheek. It was an act of complete benevolence that I have never forgotten. Not a word was exchanged. He had spoken with his eyes and made me feel stronger.

My friends prayed the evening service with us. This act of drawing us into a circle of accustomed devotions and chants soothed and comforted. They did not linger too long—another practical measure that visitors to a house of mourning ought to consider. As with most things, your instincts will tell you what to say or not say, when to come and when to leave. Stay only as you are needed; it is not a social occasion.

Don't ask questions of bereaved people without the context of truly knowing them and the one they have lost.

Regardless of how people help or don't help in the days after a funeral, their presence, in some ways, also creates a bubble. It is therapeutic and valuable, and we are helped to transition because of it, but it is also a kind of buffer. That is to say, we don't really quite confront the hard wall of the truth until everyone has finally left the house on the last day of the agreed period at home.

Be prepared for the thud of harsh loneliness when the door is shut for last time and the final visitor has departed. This is one of the toughest moments—life has to resume, we must return to work, and we are required to realign to living with a hole in the soul.

In its Patient and Visitor Guide, the Mayo Clinic states: "Experts advise those grieving to realize they can't control the process and to prepare for varying stages of grief. Understanding why they're suffering can help, as can talking to others and trying to resolve issues that cause significant emotional pain, such as feeling guilty for a loved one's death. Mourning can last for months or years. Generally, pain is tempered as time passes and as the bereaved adapts to life without a loved one."

So I believe the end of the immediate bereavement period, however it is experienced, is a useful opportunity to take a deep breath and examine your emotional situation. What do you now feel? Why do you find yourself in denial about what happened? Why do you then feel bursts of anger against her—angry that she died and left you in this predicament? How do you stop feeling guilty that he died and you're still here? These are all normal and necessary stages in the grieving cycle, but they still really hurt. If you feel it is necessary, you may wish to seek professional guidance and community support.

Most bereavement specialists concur that those suffering through loss must truly consider if the sorrow and the pain have the potential to or have already robbed them of their ability to function in the normal activities of daily life. It's difficult to self-evaluate such a thing, and it is advised to let family and trusted friends help you with their candor and compassion. While we all grieve individually, there are few who would not benefit from grief counseling and/or participation in a well-established grief support group during the weeks and months following a death.

Even though most American therapists and clinicians are busy with packed schedules of clients and patients, there remains for many people a general inclination not to visit with a psychologist after a death. Emotional issues, trouble with children, divorce, job crises, or general depression and anxiety drive Americans to psychologists and psychiatrists—with death, not so much. The stigma of being unable to just "get on with things" is all too often invoked, along with the American tendency toward stoicism and repudiation. We believe that we should be brave, and we tend to refute any suggestion that we can't get right back into our careers and social lives. But as Viktor Frankl, a psychiatrist and survivor of the Nazi concentration camps, wrote: "When we are no longer able to change a situation, we are challenged to change ourselves."[16] So it is with grief; it forces us to adjust.

I remember only weeks after my father died, our family convened at the house for the annual Seder, the festive banquet of Passover. My father had always proudly led and meticulously directed the ceremonial meal, holding, reading, and chanting from the *Haggadah*, the book of blessings and folksongs that also includes the grand narrative of the exodus of the Hebrew slaves from Egypt. Like a provincial king, he raised his glass of wine at every appropriate juncture in the service around the carefully organized table. He imperiously broke the outsized communal *matzah* in half to signify the strenuous human journey to freedom.

16 Viktor E. Frankl, *Man's Search for Meaning* (New York: Washington Square Press, 1962).

It was Passover for me, Christmas for some, and Eid al-Fitr for still others. Regardless of creed, we all have bittersweet memories of a parent or grandparent who was the principal figure at holiday gatherings and with whose voice, face, and hands we associate the occasion.

Naturally, it was difficult to gather for the celebration so soon after we lost the given leader of this hallowed dinner-table event. The bitter herbs we always tasted at the meal especially stung our throats, and the saltwater, representing the tears of enslaved peoples, drained into our souls. And, at the outset, there was the question of who would now sit in Dad's chair and conduct the rite. Although I am the elder of three children, I deferred to my brother, Sam. Sam was sixteen and his suffering was pronounced; he had especially adulated our father.

Sam solemnly reached into the dining room cabinet to retrieve the *Haggadah* books with the mournful gravity of a curator in a private museum. He distributed them reverently to all of us, including our sobbing mother. The room filled with an elegiac stillness.

I realized quickly that I had been serendipitously handed a distinct *Haggadah*, indeed. It was the one my father had used for all those years. Sighing to myself, I saw his handwritten commentary in the book, along the margins. In a quiet shock of recognition, I observed his slanted, Semitic scrawling in the myriad, fussy notes to himself. Dad had, over the course of time, and beholden to his honored responsibility, jotted down an entire personal guide of data, instructions, comments, and directions that he used in conjunction with the text of Passover night.

Later, at one point in the Seder, Sam became momentarily flustered. He wasn't altogether certain how to proceed. Some *Haggadah* books are heavily laden with prayers and passages; reasonable deviation and improvisation is permitted and acceptable. Our father wove his own way through the manual while leading us.

Sam looked up and indicated that he did not recall what exactly the next step would be. He glanced around the table, amiably anticipating a suggestion. I looked up from the page in my book and announced, "Sammy! He tells us what to do."

"What?" my brother asked.

"Dad is telling us what to do." Then, reading from what my father had inscribed neatly in the book, I declared, "Now turn to page 27 and ask the children to sing."

We all turned to page 27 and were soon singing, "Go down Moses to Egypt-land/ Tell old Pharaoh, let my people go!" Even my mother smiled through glistening tears as she sang out loud. Sam, our sister, and I sat in praise, feeling as though our collective shoulder had been tapped from heaven. We realized, as we spiritually took another step across the bridge of grief, that our parents would always leave their handwriting in our lives. With his peculiar, slanted script, our father was still there. All we needed to do was remember him. Not for two days, not for seven, but for always.

Chapter Five

Channeling Your Grief: What Should I Do in the First Year after a Death?

. . . .

"Grief can be the garden of compassion. If you keep your heart open through everything, your pain can become your greatest ally in your life's search for love and wisdom."
Rumi

People alleviate their grief by turning it over to creative and caring endeavors that honor and reflect the life of someone they remember. People often make a decision to do something like this about six months or so after a death. A study about grief published in 2009 by the National Institutes of Health (NIH) revealed a number of complications are created by delayed or ignored sorrow. The report indicated that about six months after a loss, in cases when survivors did not face the reality of death and did not endure bereavement, serious psychological risks were at play.

What happens is sometimes called "complicated grief." An NIH report states:

> People with complicated grief are at risk for cancer, cardiac disease, hypertension, substance abuse, major

depression, posttraumatic stress disorder, and suicidal thoughts and actions. Complicated grief, a syndrome that occurs in about 10 percent of bereaved people, results from the failure to transition from acute to integrated grief. As a result, acute grief is prolonged, perhaps indefinitely. Symptoms include separation distress (recurrent pangs of painful emotions, with intense yearning and longing for the deceased, and preoccupation with thoughts of the loved one) and traumatic distress (sense of disbelief regarding the death, anger and bitterness, distressing, intrusive thoughts related to the death, and pronounced avoidance of reminders of the painful loss).[17]

Bereavement and Unresolved Grief

A social worker named Judy Tatelbaum wrote a book in 1980 called *The Courage to Grieve*. The author expressed that after someone dies, "[W]e must thoroughly experience all the feelings evoked by our loss," and if we don't, "problems and symptoms of unsuccessful grief" will occur. In fact, the concern that people who experience a death must actively undertake their feelings, clinically or therapeutically, or otherwise suffer post-traumatic issues, originated with Sigmund Freud. The Viennese neurologist was, arguably, the original scientific scholar to identify both the significance and the *pervasiveness* of unresolved grief. He began to concentrate on bereavement while living through World War I.

Like many, Freud was deeply shaken by the frightful number of people—military and civilian—who perished during the war. It is estimated that eighteen million people were killed. Several million of these died from disease and pandemics. Death became the center of a new and morbid universe. The *Encyclopedia of Death and Dying*

---

17 Sidney Zisook and Katherine Shear, "Grief and Bereavement: What Psychiatrists Need to Know, *World Psychiatry*, https://www.ncbi.nlm.nih.gov/pmc/articles/PMC2691160.

reports: "Many of Freud's family members and friends were suffering from depression, agitation, physical ailments, and suicidal thoughts and behavior. Later he realized that many people lived in grief for deaths not related to the war and that these losses might account for their various emotional and physical problems. Freud's grief-work theory suggested the importance of expressing grief . . . in order to recover full function."[18]

Freud referred to death as "the great unknown" and "the gravest of all misfortunes." He became committed to equating death and grief because until the cataclysm of the Great War, people simply did not think about it all that much. Before his era, there had been little scientific or clinical study of death and grief because, thought the psychoanalyst, people were more interested in things they had actually known, such as love, hunger, sexual desire, spiritual ecstasy, or having children. Humans were not inclined to fear death because, ironically, they had never had this experience and because, as he asserted, finality and death are simply not computed by the unconscious. We are in denial, which is dangerous. We need grief, which is remedial.

Freud introduced revolutionary concepts about death. He called it "the aim of life" and he declared, "everyone owes nature a death." He demanded we all become *consciously aware* of it. It may be strange to us now, who watch death twenty-four/seven on television and social media, but until about the twentieth century and its genocides, death was largely a private and singular matter and grieving was hardly examined from the medical and psychological viewpoints. In fact, to this day, there remains a limited amount of study about death and bereavement in the curricula of many medical schools. Physicians know a great deal biologically about death but not nearly as much about how survivors cope in light of a death.

18 *Encyclopedia of Death and Dying*, http://www.deathreference.com/En-Gh/Freud-Sigmund.html#ixzz4dWhCn6Sx, accessed September 2017.

I think Freud is really the one who discovered "complicated grief." He became preoccupied with mortality and mourning in the latter part of his life and career—particularly as Nazism spread in Germany and Europe was sliding into a second inferno. Freud was a Jew and his publications were conspicuous among the books that were burned and banned by the Hitler regime. He and his family escaped from Austria in 1938, fleeing to London—where he died on September 23, 1939, just as World War II and the Holocaust of European Jewry were breaking out.

Freud's youngest child, Anna, was also an acclaimed psychoanalyst; her work focused on children. She nursed and cared for her father as he was succumbing to jaw cancer. Anna responded to her father's death in a way worth noting—remembering his deep concern for the suffering of youngsters caused by warfare, she created a foster care center in London. The mission worked to save and rehabilitate the city's children from the continuing bombardment of German rockets and bombs. The "Hampstead War Nursery" proved effective and cured many little ones from their wounds, both physical and emotional. After the war, it was revamped into a healing center for youngsters who had survived the Nazi concentration camps.

We who survive the death of a loved one can gain much inner strength and therapeutic relief by turning our grief into expressive, imaginative, or philanthropic work in our loved one's name. It's particularly redemptive in situations of complicated grief. Again, as the prayer book says, "Grief is a great teacher, if it sends us back to serve the living."[19]

Channeling Grief

Three years after his teenage son took his own life, his father spoke to me about the anti-suicide mentoring foundation he created in his memory. He was by then freed from the immediate grief, which he had

19 *Gates of Prayer* (New York: Central Conference of American Rabbis, 1975).

processed through with support groups, his church, and a number of bereavement therapists. The scar will always be there, but the father was now reflective and philosophical about his family's situation. He managed to turn his grief into healing by turning the memory of Tobey into the future of many other young people.

He told me that what had helped him was the opportunity to make a difference in the lives of these other youngsters. "They are all vulnerable," he said. "Each time we help one of these kids, I feel my son closer and closer to me. And it keeps his memory alive because we teach these high schoolers all about Tobey's values, his struggles, and his wonderful optimism."

The dad made it clear that in recovering from his complicated grief, he discovered a beneficial values clarification. Time and work were no longer dominating him—he had taken charge of both. He spoke to me about his new definition of time, "I have learned to really honor time and the use of it. It's not about money anymore for me. You can lose money or valuables, but time misspent just vanishes."

Countless numbers of people have channeled their emotional wounds after losing someone—particularly in tragic situations—into foundation and charitable work in favor of life and progress. Among the most renowned is John Walsh, who lost his six-year-old son Adam to a brutal abduction and murder. Walsh is well-known for hosting the long-running television program, *America's Most Wanted*, which has steered the rescue and recovery of scores of missing children. He and his wife, Revé, established the Adam Walsh Child Resource Center, a not-for-profit association that has directly led to several laws being passed to help locate and support the young victims of pedophiles and child molesters.

Walsh appears muscular and commanding on television. He is a household name. But even his powerful persona cannot conceal his unrelenting pain. His cause, however, has given that pain substantial therapeutic release. He has stated, "People don't understand the devastation the murder of a child does to someone. Eighty percent of parents of murdered children wind up in divorce. The only thing you have in common is that horrible sadness. You can't see the joy of your previous life."

Similarly, the family of Polly Klaas has turned their tragedy into triumph by creating the Polly Klaas Foundation, which is also dedicated to child safety and recovery. Polly was snatched from a pajama party in her California home and murdered in the fall of 1993. Her mother was quoted two weeks after Polly's disappearance, "I have a daughter out there—without shoes."[20] This anguished plea from a mother galvanized the nation into a new awareness of the horrors of abducted children. The foundation inspired the enactment of "Amber Laws" in all fifty states.

The name Susan G. Komen is synonymous with breast cancer awareness. The foundation was founded in 1982 by Komen's sister, Nancy, after Susan died from the disease at the age of thirty-six. Nancy made a promise to her dying sister that she would do everything possible to eradicate breast cancer and its attendant agony, humiliation, and dread. Komen, as the organization is simply called, has changed the entire medical culture of breast cancer, with its five-kilometer Race for the Cure and other fitness walks, its national hotline, meal deliveries, and free mammograms and surgeries for those afflicted.

Although grief is personal, it sometimes is even bigger than the person who is grieving. Soldiers who've outlasted war nonetheless directly witnessed close comrades being blown to bits and were splattered by their friends' blood and body tissue. Men, women, and children who have outlived the numerous genocides and ethnic cleansings of both the twentieth and twenty-first centuries are

---

20 "Polly's Story," published by the Polly Klaas Foundation, www.pollyklaas.org.

plagued by punishing trauma, terrifying dreams, and, of course, their devastating sorrow for their family members who were slaughtered.

Private bereavement is hard enough. But when death is experienced as part of a massive, horrific event or cataclysm, the consequences and suffering are unimaginable. That is why we can learn so much from the coping mechanisms of such survivors.

In the spring of 1979, I joined with a group of fellow clergy in Toronto to welcome an uncommonly unique visitor over a luncheon discussion. A tragic man named Otto Frank appeared in the room. At ninety years of age, eternally bowed with sorrow, he nonetheless held his firm physique with elegiac gravitas. He was impeccably outfitted, true to his Swiss-German businessman's roots, all but bald, and with a neatly trimmed moustache. His eyes emitted no light and his mouth was a wound.

Otto Frank, who would die a year later in Switzerland, was the father of Anne Frank—the hauntingly passionate teenage diary writer and poet laureate of the Nazi Holocaust. Otto's family of four hid in "the secret annex" above his business office at Prinsengracht 263 in Amsterdam for two years during the Second World War. They were ultimately betrayed by an outsider and arrested by the Gestapo in 1944.

The family was brutally dispersed among the concentration camps. Fifteen-year-old Anne died of typhus in Bergen-Belsen just weeks before British soldiers liberated the camp. Her older sister Margot also perished in the camp within days of Anne. The final whereabouts and fate of their mother, Edith, were never discovered. Otto managed to endure several months in the hell of Auschwitz and was liberated at the war's end. He immediately made his way back to Amsterdam and reconnected with a sympathetic couple, Jan and Miep Gies, who were among the small group of "Righteous Gentiles" who helped conceal the Franks and who smuggled food, clothes, and books to them. Miep Gies had been Otto's private secretary. She and all those collaborators, who risked their lives to assist the Franks and four others in the secret attic, were the group's only contact with the outside world for more than two years.

Otto Frank now sat down among us looking like a stone. A priest asked him, "Mr. Frank, how did you cope with the loss of your family?" The older man closed his eyes for a few moments and then opened them. Slowly, deliberately, he spoke in strongly accented English:

"I don't know that I truly coped. What I know is they are all gone and I am still here. What gave me strength was the discovery of Annie's diary."

Miep Gies was the one who found the plaid, cloth-covered journal kept judiciously by the teenage Anne Frank. Gies had wandered mournfully through the cramped, four-room annex just after its Jewish internees were removed. When Otto Frank returned to Amsterdam, he sought out Miep and she gave him the diary, which has become one of the world's best-selling books.

Otto Frank told us that day in 1979 that he had never realized how deep and sensitive his younger daughter was. Years before, he stated:

> I began to read slowly, only a few pages each day, more
> would have been impossible, as I was overwhelmed by
> painful memories. For me, it was a revelation. There, was
> revealed a completely different Anne to the child that I
> had lost. I had no idea of the depths of her thoughts and
> feelings.[21]

The diary uncovered someone transcendent who he had not known. His daughter was a feminist: "I know that I am a woman, a woman with inward strength and plenty of courage." She was an inspirational messenger: "Everyone has inside of him a piece of good news. The good

---

21 Posted and on display at the Anne Frank House and Museum in Amsterdam. Also online at http://www.annefrank.org/en/Anne-Frank/Otto-returns-alone/Otto-reads-Annes-diary.

news is that you don't know how great you can be! How much you can love! What you can accomplish! And what your potential is!"

And then came what is arguably the most renowned and poignant paragraph written by Anne Frank, the idealist and optimist:

> It's difficult in times like these: ideals, dreams and cherished hopes rise within us, only to be crushed by grim reality. It's a wonder I haven't abandoned all my ideals, they seem so absurd and impractical. Yet I cling to them because I still believe, in spite of everything, that people are truly good at heart.[22]

Otto Frank was able to have *The Dairy of a Young Girl* published in 1947, and it has been translated into sixty languages. Eleanor Roosevelt wrote the introduction to the English language edition. In so many ways, Anne Frank has never died.

Turning his indescribable grief into creative tribute—as well as his feelings of guilt over surviving what destroyed his entire family—Otto Frank dedicated the remaining decades of his life to spreading Anne's story and testimony throughout the globe. On the day he visited us clergy in 1979, he mentioned seeing young people in Africa and Asia reading and studying Anne Frank's diary in schools. It was the only time Otto Frank smiled that day, but it was a bright and enduring smile.

Honoring the Dead

You don't have to be or attain a high profile in order to nurse your grief with this kind of a resourceful and life-giving response to the loss of your loved one. Just as there is so much anonymous suffering in the world, as people die and other people mourn, there is also an overwhelming amount of anonymous kindness. The Hebrew Scripture encourages us: "Therefore, choose life!" Every day, turning their grief into curative work, children honor their departed parents, siblings

22 Anne Frank, *The Diary of a Young Girl* (New York: Doubleday, 1967).

venerate their siblings, and, yes, parents exalt their children. In their memory and in tribute to what they believed or championed, gardens are planted, churches refurbished, benches or bricks sponsored, modest charitable funds created, library collections started, street sections "adopted," volunteer projects begun, or food and clothing donated. There is no greater antidote for grief than service to the living that reflects the values and principles of someone we so keenly miss.

Aaron was a hearty, heavy-shouldered man with kind eyes and sturdy, work-worn hands. He laughed whenever folks in his lakeside Midwestern town called him "the Jewish carpenter." I served the community's small liberal synagogue for a brief period many years ago; Aaron and his wife, Rita, were active members. They were of humble financial means but carried a great deal of moral currency. Rita undertook many committees—from the volunteers who visited the sick in hospitals to the day care group who looked after little ones while their parents attended our religious services. Aaron, strapping and always in cheerful good spirits, contributed his time and skills enthusiastically as the synagogue "handyman." He was most revered as the annual builder of the synagogue's *sukkah*—the large booth with a thatched roof in which we gathered and where we prayed, sang, and shared joyful meals during the fall harvest festival called *Sukkot*.

Aaron's communal hut was spacious, leafy, and filled with hanging fall fruits, dried squash, and corn stalks. The autumn sunlight came through its perforated walls of pine branches, some drop cloth, bamboo reeds, and two-by-fours. The construction of the *sukkah* was Aaron's trademark, his yearly righteous deed, and he was totally identified with it.

Aaron and Rita had been married over forty years when he contracted pancreatic cancer. I would visit him at home during his final weeks, late in a particularly oppressive and steamy summer. He was thinking about the fall time *sukkah* but realized that he might not have the strength to build it. He asked me if I thought he'd make it to the holiday. I replied, "I don't know if you will make it to *Sukkot*, Aaron, but *Sukkot* will definitely make it to you."

Rita meticulously cared for her man; he wanted to die at home. One morning, I arrived a bit early and he wasn't quite up yet. When she heard him stirring, she got up to go into their bedroom. "Come join me, Rabbi Ben. He will love seeing you again."

As we entered, Aaron was sitting up in bed, smiling in warm greeting. I leaned over, took one of his big hands, and kissed his forehead. Rita came around the other side of the bed and asked him, "Aaron, are you ready for me to take care of your mouth?"

The phrase struck me. She was referring to brushing his teeth for him and helping him rinse with mouthwash. But it was so dear and direct. I sat by as she used a little basin for the ritual and a fresh, moist cloth to gently wash his face. *For love is as strong as death*, I thought to myself, reciting the verse from Ecclesiastes in my head.

Aaron died the next day. When Rita called to tell me, she almost immediately asked me between sobs, "Who will build the *sukkah* this year, Rabbi?" I responded, "We all will. He'll inspire us." And a number of the congregants did indeed assemble at the designated spot the day before the festival and we helped each other construct the familiar booth. "They needed a *sukkah*-builder in heaven," I declared during a brief memorial in the course of the work gathering. "So of course, the angels called Aaron."

But Rita had a terribly difficult time in the ensuing weeks and months. She had retired from teaching at a junior college and, without Aaron to look after, struggled with what to do during the day. The grief was withering her soul. Notably, about six months after Aaron's death, she told me that even visiting with a psychologist wasn't particularly helping. And, like some people, she simply wasn't comfortable with the idea of a support group as it did not appeal to her rather private sensibilities. She was deeply sad during the day, unable to function, and suffered from insomnia at night. She cried out to me, "I miss him *so much*! Sometimes, I don't see a point in living."

This was, of course, alarming to hear. I asked her, "You are discussing that feeling with the psychologist, right?"

"Yes, yes. Don't worry. I'm not going to kill myself. I just don't know what to do."

"What do you suppose Aaron would want you to do?"

"Ha!" Rita actually chuckled while wiping tears off her face. "I know he wouldn't want me to be like this."

We talked a while longer. She reminisced about her husband, especially at his delight in being the synagogue's *sukkah*-maker. "He really did think of it as a shelter of sorts," Rita shared with me. "He loved seeing people, especially the young people, comforting each other in it, singing songs, and breaking bread."

I said, "You know, Aaron had a lot of friends in this congregation and in this town. They really loved him. Do you mind if I talk with some of them about an idea you just gave me?"

"What idea? You have to tell me that before you talk to people. We . . . I don't have a lot of money."

"Don't worry about that," I assured her.

"So what are you thinking?"

"I'm thinking that Aaron really loved giving shelter and sanctuary to others. And, as you say, it was clear that he really loved kids. This town has a lot of youngsters who are hanging out in the streets too much and getting into trouble. Maybe we could start a youth shelter of some kind in Aaron's memory, a place they could gather and get something to eat and talk with others, including a few adult counselors, about life and other teen challenges. And you'd be in charge of running it. After all, you are a teacher, right?"

Within just weeks, with the help and input of several members of the community who were thrilled to participate, the Aaron Schechtman Welcome House was opened on the downtown strip. A small cadre of professionals and volunteers rotated in the tasks of maintaining the center, creating after-school and weekend social programming, offering free confidential discussions and advice, cooking meals, and generally reaching out to youngsters in need. Rita was there most days, baking brownies, stirring a large canister of hot bean soup, and tendering remedial tutoring in reading and writing skills. A few local corporations eventually pitched in with vending machines, snack foods, a soda station, new furniture, a sound system, and generally underwriting the place in exchange, of course, for the use of their logos on the machines, the soda and coffee cups, and the donated reading materials.

In the fall, at the second *Sukkot* holiday following Aaron's death, some of the socially challenged kids who frequented the Welcome House came and helped the synagogue committee build the *sukkah*. Rita spoke at a lectern set up on the site. Erect and proud, her eyes shining, she said, "Aaron would be so happy to see this diverse and united crowd working here today. He loved people, especially people mixing together for a common good. And Rabbi, I must correct something you said last year at this time when we were here. You said the angels needed Aaron. No, in fact, *we* need him here. My husband lives!"

Volunteers of all ages, faiths, and backgrounds rebuild the Aaron Schechtman Sukkah every year. Rita remains busy and sleeps well at night. She turned her grief into a sanctuary, and people were served.

Getting Up Close to Grief

A few months after my father died, I fell into a pronounced melancholy. One of the things we discover after a death is that other people drift away from us and cannot attend to us as they did in the immediate aftermath of the loss. This is understandable. They have their own lives and their own troubles. They don't mean to be insensitive or apathetic to our continuing anguish—through its various stages—but they have to move on as well. My Uncle Moshe had to return to Israel and look after his own immediate family and to his professional work. My friends and classmates could only listen to my lamentations for so long. In short, I was more and more solitary with my grief, and feeling very lonely.

Before the massive myocardial infarction felled my dad, I never gave much thought to heart disease. I had also been spared a lot of severe sorrow because the deaths of family members had always taken place far away—a fateful aerogramme or a harrowing phone call from my birth land of Israel amounted to the full encounter. The sudden death of another one of my uncles earned us only a brief and bitter telegram from Tel Aviv. I spent hardly any time visiting sick relatives, either at home or in the hospital, and gave proportional consideration to the issues of health and well-being.

This isolation from and lack of experience with mortality likely contributed to my tremendous inability to adjust to my father's abrupt demise. I was drifting through life and graduate school and a new marriage and really had nowhere to alight. I couldn't accept the blunt reality as depression and listlessness enveloped my spirit.

Someone made a suggestion: I should volunteer as a student-chaplain in the cardiac section of one of the city hospitals. "It'll be good for you," I was told. "Your dad succumbed to a heart attack. Go and talk to men who are dealing with coronary disease. You will discover an outlet for your pain. And it will certainly be good for the people you visit."

I did it. I reported to a hospital where the administrative staff warmly accepted my offer of service. At first, though I proudly donned a laminated "VOLUNTEER" badge, which immediately made me feel connected to a community, I was somewhat apprehensive. The heart monitors and their ominous beeping, the blood pressure pumps, the oxygen machines, the white smocks worn by the medical staffers, all made me initially feel anxious and hesitant. I kept seeing my dad in the ashen faces and slumped shoulders of many of the patients. I thought I experienced chest pains (they were psychosomatic) and had to ward off fleeting moments of panic.[23] My father's open grave flashed before my eyes. I felt myself physically holding up my broken brother Sam over the gaping hole in the earth, the plain pine box just beneath us, as he and I recited the ancient memorial prayer, the *kaddish*. Each word of the Aramaic devotion came out of Sam's mouth as a guttural cry. I saw my little sister, her blonde locks flying, as my mother-in-law walked her by the tombstones, just down the hill, a safe distance from the terror.

But by my second or third visit to the ward, I began to relax. My immediate dread yielded to an overwhelming sense of affinity and purpose. I lingered longer with each of the ailing and recovering patients and, obviously, they were now more comfortable with the more "present" me. I didn't just stand by their beds and breeze through the visits. I sat down next to them in a chair or on the side of their bed. I got up close.

Some of them, though not all, began to open up to me with their stories and their own apprehensions. I saw something of my father in them. I listened to them, recited prayers with them, which I had been denied an opportunity to share with my dad. I literally felt the grip of grief loosen for me in this work and this privilege. It was all a balm and, as I touched the gentlemen's hands or gave them sips of water or read to them, my father's inexplicable disappearance transformed into a soothing closeness with his spirit.

23 Twenty-two years later, when I reached the age my father was when he died, I endured an extended period of imagined chest pains and other illusory symptoms of cardiovascular disease. Eventually a psychotherapist diagnosed me to have a case of "cardiac neurosis." Grief can seize a person's mind down the road of life; those who've lost someone close to a particular disease are advised to anticipate this kind of delayed reaction related to numerical age.

Then there was Mr. Washofsky. He was suffering from chronic heart failure. One of the nurses told me, "We are just trying to keep him alive as long as we can." Mr. Washofsky was wiry and bespectacled, with dancing eyes and an impossibly appealing personality. He was also foreign-sounding, like my father, which was probably one of the reasons I sought to spend time with him.

"So who are you?" asked the sixtyish man, whose pale complexion and thin white hair made him look even older. His gleaming eyes betrayed his fears; however, they invited me in. It was clear that the sweet man was intensely lonely.

"I'm a student rabbi, Mr. Washofsky. From the Hebrew Union College. I came to visit you and see how you are doing. My name is Ben."

"Never mind, Ben. A rabbi, eh? You look like a kid." The man shifted his weight in the bed, heaving a bit with what sounded like an unfinished Yiddish groan. The tubes in his nose fluttered about dangerously as he lifted himself up a bit to give me a closer look.

"Yeah, you're a kid," he breathed out and fell softly back on his pillow. "A kid like you back in Warsaw (which he pronounced "Var-saw") would be pulling wood on a wagon! Ha! Ha!"

I felt a distinct concern as Mr. Washofsky guffawed; he enjoyed himself but his various monitors were getting busy. I took a step toward him but he continued to observe and chat.

"From de Hebrew Union, eh? A Reform rabbi they send me. De ones that don't have time for de traditions. Oy, I need a prayer or two, even from de Reform!"

He was teasing me and I was totally charmed by this Polish man. His crusty good nature was disarming, and I felt something warm inside drawing me to his face that seemed now a touch more possessed of color.

"Yes, de Reform," I retorted with mimicry. He smiled and I chuckled. Then he shut his eyes momentarily and let out a long breath.

"Oh, vat's de difference? *Vat's de difference?* Reform. Orthodox. Vatever. Jew. Gentile. Does God really care? I accept your kindness, young man. Excuse me, Mr. Student Rabbi. So what do you have to say? Nice of you to be here. My son is in California, older than you, I think. A pretty good job he got himself with a company that sells, eh, brochures, something like dat, to de car dealerships. Something like that, what do I know? I had three heart attacks already. My wife is already dead, what can I do? What's your name, Mr. Student Rabbi?"

"Uh, Ben. I told you before."

"So it kills you to mention it again?" Then he asked me where I was from. I said, "From right here, actually, Cincinnati."

"Vat are you talking?" The old man roared. "Nobody is from Cincinnati! Nobody is from America, either! You know vat I'm talking? Come on, where is your father from?"

There was a little ripple in my chest as he mentioned my father. But I answered, "My father was from Israel, Mr. Washofsky. And actually, you're right. I'm not from Cincinnati, either. I was born in Israel also."

"Israel? That's something. I keep telling my son—did I mention he got divorced already? What can I say? What can I do? Divorced, like a bullet! I keep telling him, with de car brochures, I say, 'Take your kids, go see Israel.' That's a place. That's a beauty."

"Were you there, Mr. Washofsky?"

"Never."

He was actually playing me now. And I knew that this rascally old man, in his final few weeks on earth, was relishing being himself.

"Okay. Uh, you have now many grandchildren, Mr. Washofsky?" I suddenly heard myself speaking with an affected Eastern European inflection. I imagine now, as I looked for my father in Mr. Washofsky's bed, that I could not find enough ways to pay tribute to this funny gentleman with a fickle heart muscle.

"Vell, I have two little grandchildren. You never seen such babies. California sees them, I don't. But whenever I do, let me tell you. Dat is life for me, dat tells me I'm still alive! You know vat I'm talking?"

I looked at Mr. Washofsky who, I learned later, had survived a fourteen-month internment at Auschwitz. I was so grateful to have met him and hear his brimming passion for his grandchildren. Now I asked him, "When are you going to see your grandchildren again?"

He lit up. "Actually, soon. He's bringing them soon, he says, the brochures salesman. He comes with them every time I have a heart attack! Ha-ha!" Mr. Washofsky let out a chopping cough and the flimsy bedframe shook. "Take it easy!" I pleaded, grabbing his narrow wrists and noticing the concentration camp tattoo number on his forearm. "You must remember your strength. You should preserve yourself for your children."

Mr. Washofsky looked me straight in the eye.

"Vere did you read dat line, in a rabbi book?"

He is more than a fond recollection; that endearing heart patient I visited in the months after my father died. He had no idea, juggling memory and mischief in his simple hospital bed, trying to come to terms with his son's considerable absence from the situation, how he lifted my soul and moved me further across the bridge of grief. Mr. Washofsky became president *emeritus* of my own spiritual memorial foundation. And whenever I recall him, I whisper to myself, with gratitude, "For grief is a great teacher, if it sends us back to serve and bless the living."

Chapter Six

Necessary Business:
What Does the Funeral
Director Think, Say, and Do?

. . . .

"The purpose of life is not to be happy. It is to be useful,
to be honorable, to be compassionate, to have it make
some difference that you have lived and lived well."
Ralph Waldo Emerson

QUIET PLEASE
Service in Progress

The sign, though momentarily off to the side, remained visible as I entered the foyer of the Saidler-Dunn Memorial Chapel, a respected mortuary that was nonetheless barely noticeable along the suburban boulevard. A somber, pale building without fanfare, it blended unceremoniously into the long and typically American thoroughfare of doughnut shops, fried chicken eateries, golden arches, auto repair centers, franchised drug stores, and chain retail outlets. My fellow clergy and me try to create requiem solemnity in places like Saidler-Dunn. During funerals, we eulogize, we bless human lives, we invoke God's name, and then we often get into a parade of waxed cars and limousines and drive to the cemeteries along the wrapper-strewn avenues of the eternal test-market culture.

Meanwhile, in this particular funeral home that attends to the local Jewish community, I am greeted by a well-built bearded man, with kind eyes, named Emanuel Steinbock. His wool suit and silk tie, both charcoal-colored, blend impeccably. Manny, as he is called, has been a licensed funeral director since 1987, and this building is his primary workplace. After pleasant handshakes, we settle into his somewhat cramped office, and I ask Manny about his work.

His response is immediate. "It is all-consuming and has a great emotional and physical impact on me." He proceeds to explain the burden that transfers to him after any death. "To arrange a funeral generally involves ten to twelve hours," he says. Manny notes the extensive coordination required each and every time among family members, clergy, his funeral staff, and the cemetery administration. All this happens in the environment of fresh grief.

"But first, they call the funeral director," he emphasizes. "There is a trained person here in this building twenty-four hours a day. We don't have or believe in an answering service. Deaths occur at all times. I am phoned at all hours, day or night. Our job is to immediately give survivors reassurance and then organize the next few days of their lives."

Manny is responsible for retrieving and transporting the body from wherever it is, for writing and releasing obituary notices for the press and web, for establishing which religious rites are applicable, and for arranging the death certificate. Will there be a viewing of the body prior to the service? Will the grave be ready in a timely fashion? Is there going to be a protective vault involved in addition to the casket?

"Funerals are for the living," Manny accentuates. The living, acknowledging their dead, come to see him in this same office. "The members of the family," he says, "are confronting a lot of things. Some of them don't have as much experience with this as others do. I have to explain and propose religious rituals to them, and they don't always agree with each other."

Manny recounts that a woman had just been in earlier, along with her adult son. Their husband and father had succumbed to Parkinson's disease. "The woman was quite negative on religion. But the son, like many children at such a time, needed religion. I worked out a series of compromises that I hope will satisfy both of them in their grief."

As we converse, Manny often gestures toward the empty couch between us. Numerous dramas occur on and around this piece of furniture. A perch for despairing persons, it was wrinkled with emotions, stained by tears, bent by anger, pressed for secrets. "I've seen a lot of things in here," says the seasoned funeral director, his eyes flashing with wisdom. A purveyor of pathology, microbiology, social security law, accounting principles, veteran benefits, and biohazard wastes, Manny Steinbock is ultimately a manager of mortality, a human coda in a society increasingly unaccustomed to limits.

Manny regards his vocation with sensitivity, and he listens carefully to the people he services. He is affected when they cry, and he is attentive when they bewail. Is this exceptional in the mortuary business? While there is a great deal of skepticism, even cynicism, out there about this industry, I believe that, like in any other field, there are principled professionals at work and there are others who are devoid of high standards or even an awareness of the gravity of the situations they are managing. More than one funeral director has conceded this inconsistency to me. We are a vogue-driven culture; some funeral establishments wouldn't be proffering sailboat-style coffins or cremation urns that are shaped like reading lamps unless we as consumers weren't responding to these odd retail tactics. At the same time, I clearly remember when I completed a course for certification as a "pre-needs" counselor,[24] I saw and heard some unsavory things.

The very first day, even before the session began, the recruiter for this program pulled me aside and told me, "Look, you can't make any deals with the people you are selling a funeral or a grave or a casket, whatever. There's no negotiating. They've got to have the money up front. They can't tell you there's too much on their credit card. We offer them financing but, no matter what, you don't leave without the money worked out 100 percent and that's that." While I did gain many insights during the course, which has enabled me to serve people with greater sensitivity while they journey through the grieving process, I found some of the banter among the funeral professionals distasteful and insensitive. Again, over and over again, I heard the maddening refrain, "Remember, people, the first three letters in funeral are FUN!" There is simply no context for such a flippant philosophy to exist within an enterprise that services human beings at the most tender juncture in this life.

How Does One Choose?

Before continuing our discussion in his office, Manny takes me on a tour of the facility. He glows with purpose as we enter the Death Education Library, a softly lit room just adjacent to the casket showcase chamber. The library is filled with books, pamphlets, and videos about mourning, bereavement, healing, and sharing. The director, the father of two boys, has a delicate spot in his heart for the needs of youngsters. During our visit, he frequently expressed his keen anguish about dealing with the expired bodies of children.

---

24 I did not pursue a career as a preplanner for the funeral consortium. My interest was to learn more about what people go through and how they are treated while contracting such an agreement—for my own professional edification.

Manny continues his discourse about the library. "Many of the hospice people use it; and family members who are doing the right thing, that is preplanning for a funeral." Manny then hands me an unused coloring book for kids entitled *Kolie and the Funeral.* There are "helpful hints" for grown-ups on the inside back cover; Manny often hands the book and some crayons to children experiencing the death of a loved one. It is filled with both happy and gloomy drawings of "a little koala named Kolie. One day, Kolie's mama told him that his grandpa had died."

There were subsequent sketches, to be filled in by a child's colors and emotions, of a sad koala family, a funeral home, a casket, the deceased grandfather koala at rest in his open coffin, a hearse entering the Koalaville Cemetery, the little koala visiting the grave sometime after the funeral. Manny passed this coloring book to me as though he were transferring scripture.

We enter the next area, which is a dealer-style showroom filled with coffins on display. "This is where reality hits," Manny tells me. The decorative boxes, furnished with linings and pillows, all pose opened, gaping with vacancy. In this room, terror has flared, denial has been blunted, and ultimately, deals have been closed. Manny points to a certain, particularly lavish, regal casket with a cost equivalent to that of a well-equipped automobile.

Though no stranger to caskets, I examined and touched the various models, thinking about broken people coming into this retail sales center and trying to figure out which selection is most fitting and how it can be handled financially. They experience such torment: "If I don't spend a lot for a fancier box, will Dad's legacy be slighted?" Such guilt: "I didn't even know Mom well enough to discern what she'd want for a casket." The models included Tigereye Bronze, Fawn Stainless Steel, Grecian Copper, Star Quartz, Neapolitan Blue, Revere Silver,

Emeraldtone, and entire categories of steels and hardwoods (mahogany, cherry wood, poplar, oak).

The caskets were laced with a choice of velvets, crepes, and a wide selection of stains. The least expensive were cloth-covered or plain pine (favored by Jews and Muslims). The overall price range for the coffins was from roughly $800 to multiple thousands of dollars. Several of the models were named for biblical tribes.

As in every funeral showroom I've ever visited, a legally required disclaimer appeared on the wall:

> *Neither this funeral establishment nor any of its employees represents or implies that any casket will be airtight or watertight or will provide long-term preservation of human remains.*

When we Americans grieve, we normally fall in as mortuary client-consumers, which makes us even more vulnerable. The funeral industry is a recession-proof business, and many once privately owned funeral homes, including Saidler-Dunn, have been swallowed up to become part of conglomerate chains such as Dignity Memorial (also known as SCI) or Hillenbrand, Inc. Meanwhile, Wal-Mart, the world's largest retailer, began the trend of selling low-priced caskets online. And so, our challenge is to find a compassionate human being who represents the business to us at this hardest time of our lives—Manny Steinbock being such a person.

But the best way to work with the industry, without question, is to preplan the funeral. We routinely preplan weddings, bar mitzvah ceremonies, graduations, and christenings, so why not apply this rational practice to the most excruciating milestone in life. Why not save a great deal of money and be spared all of the agonizing indecision and second-guessing that attend to a memorial that was not prearranged by the person we seek to honor?

Manny continued the tour. Also on display for discussion and sale in the showroom were examples of outer burial containers, or vaults, "so the grave does not sink in." Prices were higher for Sunday or holiday installation. I thought, in this case, that the entire presentation of a necessary and fundamental consumer operation was dignified and restrained. I couldn't think of any other way for Manny to demonstrate his goods and services. "It's in this room, with the casket they've chosen nearby, that I discuss with the family what clothes their loved one will wear," he adds.

A separate, general price list itemized the costs for an astonishing array of often-essential ministrations performed by the funeral agency. These included embalming,[25] refrigeration, bathing and handling, dressing and casketing, transferring of the body to or from airport or mortuary (night transportation was higher), floral arranging, cremation, urns, the funeral vehicle, the family limousine, the service car, shrouds, blankets, memorial books, acknowledgment cards, temporary grave markers, candles, and pallbearer gloves. "In all this," Manny notes, "we have to take precautions in handling everything. We're concerned about AIDS, hepatitis, airborne viruses. This is complicated work."

Back in his office, I ask Manny, what has his work taught him personally about mortality?

"Being all around this for so long, I don't get too excited about most things," he says. "I don't get all worked up about a dry-cleaning order, or if my landscaper didn't exactly do a great job. I may be too laid back because of what I see here and I may have a tendency to put off

25 There are people—and a few morticians—who vigorously decry embalming. They feel it is somewhat theatrical and that, for purposes of grief therapy, human corpses should actually not be made to look "alive." "A chemically preserved body looks like a wax replica of a person. Bodies are supposed to be drooping and turning very pale and sinking in while decomposing. Within a day or so after someone died, you should be able to see that this person has very much left the building. That's the point. I think dead bodies should look dead. It helps with the grieving process."—Los Angeles funeral director Caitlin Doughty, as quoted in *WIRED* Magazine, September 17, 2014.

decisions about future things. But I can't help it. It's usually not worth it. We really can't plan all that much. I think I appreciate life in a way that others possibly don't."

Manny's phone rings, startling both of us. He picks up the receiver and listens. "I'm so sorry," he says. "I'll be over shortly. I knew your father. He was a good man."

A process begins, an agency mobilizes. A life has ended, and several other lives, including that of Manny Steinbock, are about to be further illuminated.

The Care Center

More recently, a funeral director in Oceanside, California, opened a thick, code-controlled door to what is called "The Care Center" of the Eternal Hills Mortuary and Crematoria. Debbie Allen,[26] an effusively agreeable woman in her fifties, is the general manager of the site. I followed her into the stark, neatly organized room that smelled of formaldehyde, and beheld five human corpses lying on white metal tables, their lifeless faces outlined beneath sheets, their noses pointing skyward. "The Care Center" is a euphemism for the embalming room.

A preparation room, as it is also termed, is distinctly unnerving. Alan Feuer succinctly describes this room in a *New York Times* article as "a starkly lighted chamber with a tangy iron odor, a silence one can feel, and the subterranean dankness of a crypt."

Within a moment or so, a man in custodial garb came through an opposite door after clicking the password, and Debbie spoke to him. "Is that Number Four done?" she asked him, gesturing toward the body of a dark-skinned woman with a net holding her hair in place and some kind of gel visible across her sunken face. He nodded affirmatively and walked out of the room. I realized that this man was the crematory operator— the oven was in the adjoining room outside this preparation center.

26 In this case, it's her real name, and the actual memorial park in suburban San Diego.

Neither Debbie nor the operator saw anything remarkable in this sterile space that is meticulously ventilated with outside air in accordance with the Occupational Safety and Health Administration (OSHA) standards and compliance. The air inside this prep room would otherwise remain toxic and biohazardous for the embalmers. Debbie and the passing crematory operator were in their normal, daily work environment.

Debbie noticed me looking at the dead woman and explained, "The gel on her face is a hydrating fluid." During the twenty minutes or so spent with Debbie in the cramped Care Center, I did a mental itemization of an extraordinary—but necessary—inventory. The facility contained drainage tubes for blood and other body fluids, injection and aspirating devices, "stopcocks" (ball valves that control the flow of liquids or gas), trocars, scalpels, razor blades, forceps, scissors, syringes, needles, suturing supplies, plastic undergarments, cottons and fillers, cosmetics and brushes, soaps, sanitizers, deodorizers, plastic gloves, towels, sheets, pillowcases, head positioners, eye caps, and restorer waxes. Debbie readily opened almost all of the high-standing cabinet doors and pointed out the countless bottles and containers and pumps and other items maintained and catalogued assiduously.

The mainstay stock was formaldehyde. I didn't realize until this visit just how many varieties and colors of formaldehyde exist and are utilized. Debbie explained, "It depends on the shade of the skin and other internal situations that affect the coloration of the body." All the blood in each corpse was machine-drained and replaced with the carcinogenic preserving fluid.

I stepped back, still keenly aware of the five corpses that filled the room with a looming motionlessness, and realized that I was brushing against a coffin-shaped, grayish, cardboard transport box. "So there's someone in here?" I asked Debbie.

"Yes, there's someone in there. And he will be cremated tomorrow. We don't keep them in that for more than twelve hours."

Debbie went on to point out the large biohazard waste control section that was positioned prominently in the room, then the mortuary refrigerator that stood adjacent to it. The long, expansive, upright unit contained slot trays for fifty people and was equipped with a condensing unit that was air-cooled with R-22 refrigerant. "The refrigerator operates at thirty-seven degrees Fahrenheit," Debbie expounded.

Following our meeting, I checked online and saw a "Mortech" four-body refrigerator that retails for $15,299.95. That is less expensive than some of the caskets.

Debbie had shown me through the Selection Room prior to the Care Center. Unlike the casket showroom in Manny Steinbock's funeral home, in which the containers are in full display, this conference room only presented the corners of each casket variety thrust out of the warm-colored wall. Debbie told me that the displays were termed "the needed merchandise and etiquette items." This is the trend in American funeral marketing, and it does feel more discreet than an indoor parking lot of full-blown coffins. "It's much easier on people," Debbie said. "But legally," she added, pointing to a plaque-like marker on the wall, "we must still display this sign." I noticed the familiar-sounding language:

> *There is no scientific or other evidence that any casket*
> *with a sealing device will preserve human remains.*

There was an elaborate presentation of cremation urns for purchase, some traditional-looking (wood, ceramic, marble, metal), and others ranging in shape from reading lamps, birds, fish, butterflies, baseball mitts, golf clubs, harps, sewing machines, ice skates, footballs, cooking skillets, motorcycles, smoking pipes, firefighter hats, and "veteran urns"—a bronze combat helmet sealed across a pair of rough-hewn military boots. There are also biodegradable urns available, in keeping with those who are environmentally concerned.

The artistic flair and creativity of the themed urns vanished quickly when, following our sojourn in the element-controlled embalming chamber, Debbie walked me over to the crematorium. It was just outside the password-monitored door. It was noticeably warm in this space—the sliding vault-like cover of the daunting, gloomy-grayish oven was half-open, spewing a smoldering fire and end-of-days smoke. I looked inside and beheld a spread, smoldering heap of ashes and burnt bones.

"Oh," Debbie said, referring to the crematory operator, "I guess he just finished cremating somebody, so it's going to need to cool down."

"How long does this process take?" I asked.

"About two and a half hours. Yeah, it's pretty hot so he must have had three today." Debbie then showed an anteroom with a curtained window, a couple of chairs, and a couch. The window looked directly into the oven. "This is the Witness Room," she explained. "This is where the family can witness the procedure."

I was startled at first. "You mean they see the actual cremation?"

"No," Debbie answered calmly. "Just the placement of the body." We talked briefly about this moment of observing that offers loved ones the opportunity to say goodbye. I thought there was a significant amount of sensitivity in this otherwise surreal set-up. I wondered aloud to my friend if anybody did stay on and watch the incineration. She said, "We don't like them to sit in here for too long. But there are some who linger a bit." Then, referencing the Hindu and Buddhist traditions, which regularly turn to cremation, she added, "Sometimes the monks will stay here but we don't interfere with their prayers and rituals."

Then Debbie pointed to the ashes and bones that lay anonymously in the oven, indicating more responsibilities of the crematory operator. "So this one is cooling down. And then he will put it in the processor, process it, and from there he will remove it and place the remains into the selected urn[27]—you see, there are the urns lined up there. And every person, before they are cremated, has to be weighed and then they are placed on that scale you see over there and their remains have to be weighed and the difference recorded."

"This is monitored and documented very carefully?" I asked.

"Oh yes."

And then I noticed an oversized toolbox labeled, unsurprisingly, CREMATORY TOOLBOX. "Yes, there are tools there for both the prep room and crematory," Debbie said. All of the implements intermingled, all being essential for the scrupulous embalming and refurbishing, the draining and cosmetics and biohazards, and then the incineration. So it was apparent that all these critical, funereal tasks were intertwined at the mortuary—from fluids to ice to fire. And all of them inscribed in meticulous codes, formulas, and documentations.

Debbie and I now sat in her modest, impeccably tidy office. Prominent were photos of her children and grandchildren. It was late afternoon, and I asked her what kind of day she had experienced. "Fairly typical," she replied. She had spent time on the cemetery grounds, inspecting and noting any necessary repairs and landscaping issues, as well as the constant monitoring of ground sinking and water levels beneath the tombstones. There had been an "education session" that she supervised among the graves for her colleagues in the Dignity Memorial chain. She was showing properties to some of the newer sales professionals. "We have a new section of burial properties on the grounds and we just wanted to go over it and give them information on pricing, availability, casket options, permissions, and the like. It was an overview of the process. It took a couple of hours. All in the day of the life."

---

27 In 2004, the Transportation Security Administration (TSA) implemented rules for transporting urns as carry-on luggage, requiring that urns must pass successfully through the X-ray machines.

Debbie chuckled amiably, but her work is rigorous and certainly atypical. She has done it all in her thirty-plus years in the mortuary culture, from collecting the deceased from homes, hospitals, and county morgues to the intake of bereaving families, embalming, dressing of corpses, including the application of cosmetics and reshaping of collapsed jaws and smashed heads, to coordinating services, recruiting clergy, garnering death certificates and coroner permits, to overseeing burials, and comforting—even physically holding up—mourners. She has diligently learned about all the distinctions and requirements and sensibilities among myriad faith communities—Christian, Muslim, Jewish, and Eastern traditions—including the significant variations in practice among the denominations themselves. A Baptist funeral is not the same as a Catholic Memorial Mass; an Orthodox Jewish service is decidedly dissimilar, in rhythm and timing and substance, than one from the Reform branch of Judaism.

There was an occasion years ago when I particularly observed Debbie's transcendent empathy and kindheartedness. I was performing a funeral for a Sephardic Jewish family at Eternal Hills Memorial Park. The gentleman being eulogized was about to be transported from the main complex to the cemetery; it was going to be a graveside service. His widow suddenly became markedly agitated. "I forgot! I forgot!" she cried.

Both Debbie and I approached the suffering woman. Debbie put her arms around the lady and gently inquired, "What did you forget, Mrs. Gabarda? How can we help you?"

Mrs. Gabarda, her tears streaking her heavy makeup, looked at both of us. "I forgot to give you this for my husband." She held up a worn but still regal, full-sized prayer shawl, known as a *tallit*. "Can we possibly still put it on him, before he is buried?"

"Yes, of course," said Debbie.

"I want to be there when you do it," said Mrs. Gabarda. Debbie nodded toward me. She and I took the lady, clutching the old *tallit* in her hands, to a small anteroom that was adjacent to the crematorium. We strode outside the building so as to avoid any possible missteps. The three of us walked in, and Debbie, first gently eyeing the widow, opened the relatively simple coffin. Mr. Gabarda lay peacefully within. Debbie carefully took the shawl from the lady and then directed me with her eyes to help her wrap it around the man's shoulders. Mrs. Gabarda's lips trembled as we silently completed the task. She then nodded and asked, "May I say goodbye again?"

"Of course," replied Debbie. The widow leaned over and touched the *tallit* and then ran her hands across his still, bearded face. "Now you can go to God, Jacob."

Debbie is respected for both her seniority and experience, and she sometimes trains and updates her peers on matters of professionalism and best practices (legal and ethical standards) in the funeral business. She had spent a portion of the day on auditing issues and, as she put it, "putting out a couple of fires" between employees. Debbie is as firm on employee comportment as she is compassionate with grieving clients. I asked why she chose this profession and discovered, again, how people— even funeral directors—best remember others when they turn their grief into work that reflects their departed.

Debbie responded, "I got into this work because my dad died. Instead of going to nursing school, I went to mortuary college. So I've worked my way up from just working with the body aspect of it to making sure the body is well treated. My father was an alcoholic, unfortunately, with liver damage. The embalming process over thirty-five years ago was poorly done, and very difficult to take." Debbie was dismayed by the insensitivity and incompetence of the mortuary staff and made an immediate life decision. She was going to channel her grief for her father into servicing others in sorrow, making sure they did not suffer the pain she had known.

"So I made arrangements and thought, well, maybe if I sit across from somebody in the position my family was in and show compassion, show love, no matter who the deceased was, no matter how they died, who they loved, how they were loved. Showing people compassion when they are suffering. I wanted to assure them of that love and caring. I wanted them to know that I was truly with them. That I would treat them the way I wasn't treated. It was kind of a life calling for me. It's something special. You have to have patience. You have to not judge any of the families who come before you. You are here to offer them guidance and to be truthful. We are here for those whose lives have ended," Debbie declared, now almost like a prayer. "Every life has value. It's not how you start it; it's how you end it. And it's not a race. It's a journey. I believe the Lord led me to this work. God has blessed me with the opportunity of helping others."

Debbie is concerned with the tendency of Americans to sidestep the crucial steps and stages of grief. I had asked her what she observed about the American way of mourning.

"For those who have a faith," responded this reverent woman, "and believe they will see their loved ones again, what I have noticed is that they tend to let their emotions flow, which is healthy. They tend to follow the five stages of grief a bit stronger than those who don't. I believe those who don't have a faith—and even some who do—believe that grieving is some kind of weakness. That you just don't grieve. That an afterlife is a crutch. That if you show natural emotions, that if you cry, it's weakness. And I think our society does this too. 'You have to be strong,' people say. 'You are too emotional, too weak. And that's not good.' They're saying that weak people are not good. Our society prevents people from seeing value in paying tribute, in celebrating a life. And I will tell you that some people, planning their service, will just say 'Ah—put me in a pine box. Don't make a fuss.' Or they say, "Ah—just cremate me and throw my ashes out to sea.' However, that's what we *say*. But do we really mean that? We all want to be loved. We all want to be remembered. And so it's unfortunate that so many Americans tend to shun the grieving process, for different reasons, when it's so important for them and it's really what their loved ones wanted them to do."

This funeral director feels that Americans endure a lot of tribulation keeping in touch with their feelings because they just haven't made peace with humanity's impermanence. "Look, I understand. It really is hard to talk about it. It's emotional. And then it goes back to our fear of being judged as being weak if we show emotion."

Debbie picked up a photo of her grandchildren and smiled. "I'm in my late fifties. I find myself thinking about my own death. It tugs at me, of course. So I'm actually grateful when people, when they come here, are already crying. When there are tears, I know I have something to work with."

Chapter Seven

Prayerful Communication: Are There Conversations with the Dead?

· · · · · · · · · · ·

"The day which we fear as our last is
but the birthday of eternity."
Seneca

As I concluded my visit with Debbie Allen that afternoon, I asked her a last question: "Debbie, do you believe in an afterlife?"

She responded immediately, "I believe in heaven." She didn't specify what that meant but it was clear this sympathetic mortality professional trusts that there is something more to our existence than what we can see.

Just a few weeks after my father died, I lay in bed half-asleep, the clock ticking near midnight. A fragrant April breeze floated through the open windows; spring blossoms were emerging following the final frost of March. Now I felt, without a trace of trepidation, that something else flowed in with the breeze.

Looking up toward the ceiling, I saw particles of light swirling above me. It was a most consoling and soothing sight. The glowing particles, like atoms of intimacy, began to shape themselves into something. I lay and watched, feeling the presence of a commiserating medium. The lights took on a softly luminous silhouette of my father's face, suspended above the bed and me. I felt no apprehension, only great curiosity and interest.

There was no audible sound, yet I experienced the intonation of words being conveyed to me as the silhouette hovered for a moment. "I am fine and safe." The words silently penetrated my psyche and warmed my soul. The grains of light dispersed and evaporated. Only the breeze flowed through the dark room. I was filled with relief and satisfaction. I then turned over and fell into a peaceful sleep.

Encounters with Hope and Love

Writing these words now, more than forty years later, I find no second-guessing occurring in my mind. I have been with many serious, rational people who were recovering from loss and reported similar experiences. They know that life is for the living and that physical death is final and that grief must be respected and fulfilled. And yet, I remember a swirling galaxy of lights that came to me in my bedroom with my father's visage and told me not to worry about the other side.

So I was not too skeptical when Reva, an upbeat hairdresser with a firm grasp of reality, told me that her mother detects the smell of her late father's cherry pipe tobacco fumes in the house where the parents once shared life. I do not doubt that the dead have departed from us and that we must therapeutically recover from loss. But I'm not sure we can disavow the fingerprints they sometimes leave behind. Nor do I dismiss Reva's own report that, in a dream, she dialed her parents' phone number and, after no one answered on the other end of the line, she awoke with her father's voice, like a clarion, ringing in her ear: "Hello?"

· · · · · · · · · · ·

Janette is a successful writer, respected editor, and a mother who has taken life earnestly. She loved her own mother fiercely, and she took her time about getting married. In her late thirties, she first met Lenny, whom she thought was the right man, and evidently got a signal from her mother that boded well.

Sometime earlier, Marianne, Janette's mother, had been chatting with her daughter over lunch. Janette was worried about her mother, a gregarious woman who had smoked cigarettes far too long, quit too late, and was falling prey to lung cancer. Marianne was always fretting about Janette's gentlemen callers. On this occasion, she came up with an unusual criterion for Janette to consider when it came to men: "You ought to see if he ever asks you about your car."

"My car?" Janette was perplexed.

"Yes, your car. It's a practical, daily matter. A man who thinks of such things, especially with respect to his woman, is functional and wonderful. Remember that."

It was several months later, after Marianne died, that Janette met Lenny. It was late fall. While they were having dinner out together one evening, he said, "I have something to ask you."

"Okay," replied Janette.

"Tell me, have you had your car winterized yet? It's pretty important and can save you a lot of headaches and money later."

Janette blinked away her tears of joy. She felt her mother's hand on her shoulder as she looked into her future husband's face. Yes, we do hear from the dead.

But it was just after Marianne had succumbed that Janette particularly felt her mother's proximity. A few days after the funeral, Janette went to her mother's apartment—a space the two had shared on many occasions and through many crises, transitions, and milestones. This was the first time Janette would sleep alone in the apartment.

At about 4:00 in the morning, Janette awoke and went into the bathroom. "I felt a sort of cool swirl," she told me. "I couldn't discern what it was. But I felt my mother in the room with me. She was absolutely there. I didn't get scared. I didn't get upset. It felt right. I felt her essence. There wasn't exactly a sound but I heard her talking to me. She said, 'This is me. I don't want you to worry. I am here for you. I will always guide you. I will only come to you this one time but I want you to know that I am always with you.'"

"What happened then?" I asked Janette, vividly recalling my father's swirling silhouette.

"Nothing. It was a wonderful, soothing experience. I just went back to bed and felt deeply reassured."

. . . .

My folksy uncle Moshe (introduced in Chapter One and who helped me with my grief) suffered a shocking loss of his own when his second son, Uli, died. My cousin was in his mid-thirties, frolicsome and easygoing, but lived with a congenital heart defect. Uli's rather sudden demise was not altogether unexpected but it was dreadfully unsparing for his young wife and their three small children. He was truly a moderate man, soft in tone and without affectation.

On his last day on earth, Uli actually succumbed twice. He was considered technically dead early in the afternoon, and then he was miraculously revived by the medical team. He relapsed unconditionally early that evening, even as his family briefly celebrated the uncanny reprieve. But in between the coda and the curtain, Uli had told a remarkable tale to his hearkening wife.

My cousin reported that he had floated above the hospital bed and been drawn to a shining, beckoning beam of light. He told his wife that at the cusp of death, he felt a tremendous lift of air under the wings of his body. It was a wondrous sensation, he exclaimed, filled with rapture and deliverance. He then proceeded to a kind of celestial gateway. He was promptly greeted by our maternal grandfather, Samuel, for whom Uli was nicknamed. Uli described the grandfather, who preceded all of us in death, with details that were precise and familiar to only those who had known the patriarch.

Uli accurately communicated the grandfather's features, his gestures, even the timbre of his voice. There was no logical way for my doomed cousin to have known such particulars about our grandfather without having, in some way, visited with him.

Uli's heart stopped beating that evening, finally and terminally. But in between the shadows, my gentle cousin left us with a report—aside from our terrible grief—that gave us some hope.

· · · · · · · · · · ·

During his final days, as he was succumbing to esophageal cancer, Marty, my former father-in-law, spoke whimsically (in between moments of delusion and dysfunction) about taking a cross-country jaunt, by train, from Ohio to California. Who could blame the ailing man for dreaming of a journey away from himself and his predicament? We all listened to his yearning with a mixture of understanding and sadness. Then one night, about two weeks after her grandfather's death, my younger daughter Debra, a focused and reasonable teenager, ran into our house from our backyard. She was quite unsettled as she declared that she had heard a shrill train whistle while making her way toward the house. However, there simply were no railroad tracks anywhere in the vicinity of our neighborhood.

As we warily opened the back door and peered out, the porch light bulb suddenly exploded above us. We were quite relieved that no one was hit by the hot shattering glass even as we wondered what Marty was so agitated about!

What the Dead Tell Us

So, do the dead tell us things? Is there another realm? I say, yes, there is something. But it is nothing if it is all about horror and specters. For me, it can only exist in the category of hope.

In American culture, there is as much an obsession with phantasms and ghouls as there is a lack of rational thinking about life and its parameters—or possibilities. Movies and video games and sermons about vampires and demons and poltergeists and exorcisms[28] abound, all thriving on the fuel of our insecurities and fears about mortality, cemeteries, hell/heaven, and satanic dominions. The organized religions, while servicing parishioners and members with helpful liturgies and familiar rituals when people die, nonetheless tend to drive traditions of terror into our psyches. It usually has to do with issues of good versus evil, with the cycle of divine beneficence or divine retribution, or the cataclysmic tension between God and Satan. It all amounts to a theological abduction of both our therapeutic grieving cycle and the transition of our dead into eternity and some kind of peaceful afterlife.

I don't believe in ghosts; I believe in souls. This belief was sealed within me one afternoon when I literally noticed a soul departing the body of an indomitable young lady who had just lost her battle with cystic fibrosis. Sixteen-year-old Marnie Barth had lived pretty much in the children's ward of the large community hospital for two or three years. She was good-natured, funny, outgoing, and brave. She was beloved and regularly feted by the medical staff. The genetic disease

---

28 The 1973 film, *The Exorcist*, and its several sequels, had a profound effect on people. I personally witnessed a Catholic college buddy of mine literally crumble in a fearsome collapse of terror after we saw the picture. "That could happen to me!" the poor fellow kept screaming. He was ultimately sedated at a nearby emergency room.

filled and drowned her body with mucus and infections from her pancreas up through to her lungs.

I visited Marnie frequently, even as her parents and some close family friends spent endless days and nights with her during the hospital stays. The parents were still young and always hopeful, but they knew the disease would ultimately claim their child. There had been a welcome respite for a while—Marnie was spared time in the hospital, and hope grew that the illness might be in remission. But then I got a call from an aunt, "Better get down to the hospital, Rabbi. Marnie's back in and the situation is grim."

There was already a vigil in progress when I arrived. Friends and family members roamed around the ward in quiet dread. People only whispered to or simply embraced one another. Visitation in Marnie's room was restricted to one person at a time; she lay intermittently between twilight and a coma. Her mother, father, and an uncle took turns sitting with the child. I joined in the rotation so that the parents could get some rest and together time.

It was about four o'clock in the afternoon, and I happened to be in the room alone with Marnie. The attending nurse had stepped out. I looked at the girl's sad, sweet face; her long, frizzy hair was like a crown all about her head. The sound of her breathing was almost inaudible as the monitors ticked and chimed quietly and portentously. Marnie's eyes were closed. I noticed that her feeble inhalation was receding even more as her stomach made fewer and less frequent indentations under the white blanket that covered her.

Then I knew that Marnie had died. The heart machine had ceased; its screen revealed a straight, lifeless line. I momentarily was unable to swallow. I was numb and didn't know where to put my hands. Crushed by the moment, I just placed my hands under my jaw and held my head while a burst of heartache and apprehension rolled through my chest. And then at that moment—almost ineffably at first—the room filled with a calming, moist warmth, and an uncannily pleasant scent. It was something of a delicious mixture of lavender and eternity. It was fleeting, but I sensed and absorbed it; the room also briefly took on the smell of morning rain. As I stood up and looked at the peaceful child who lay before me, I saw a faint but discernible ripple underneath the blanket at the point of her abdomen. I then plainly felt and saw Marnie's soul depart her frame like an invisible little bird flying off to paradise. That is what I perceived. And then the deeply healing flash ended, and it was just Marnie and me in the sterile hospital chamber. Silence. Peace.

I edged closer and put my hand to the child's forehead. It was my own little goodbye to her. It was the gesture of reluctance about leaving the room. As long as I lingered therein, the world of Marnie's parents remained unbroken. Then I walked out of the room, and when the parents saw me, they just knew.

I was among many who helped them through the critical stages of grief, and I did not share the experience with Marnie's parents until a few days after the funeral. Her mother began to weep fresh tears but she nodded several times in a gesture of hope. Her father turned his head and stared into space. I really did not know what they thought, but I had to tell them. I felt they were entitled to know about the little bird.

· · · · · · · · · · ·

It was my duty to eulogize Dr. Joseph Tallisman one morning in the central chamber of an ornate San Diego mausoleum. The spherical, granite room, on the grounds of a tree-laden cemetery, was filled with souls, both seen and unseen. The living sat on folding chairs; the dead lay inside the walls. I spoke from behind the shiny casket at a marble podium.

I adored Joe Tallisman. He was an earnest physician of the old school. "Forgive me," he would say, "but I truly believe that a doctor needs to take care of people." I considered him youthful when he died from a stroke at the age of seventy-one. Mild-mannered and sympathetic, he exhibited a sense of calling about medicine. His smooth face, good nature, and his robust passion for the musical theater had combined to make Joe Tallisman seemingly immune to the aging process. Joe loved all the shows, from *Gypsy* to *Funny Girl* to *The Sound of Music* to—above all—*The Music Man*, starring Robert Preston.

The doctor especially liked the beat and tune of that show's paean to the town of Gary, Indiana. He knew enough about musical measures to even correctly emphasize the number's phonic accents, carefully enunciating the phrase, *"GA-ry, Indi-A-na."*

The lyrics, compositions, and show tunes of Joe's life went through my mind as I spoke his eulogy that day in the mausoleum. As the memorial service concluded, the general congregation was momentarily dismissed. Only Joe's immediate family accompanied the funeral director, the coffin, and me down a sable-colored hallway laden with leaded glass windows. We came to his crypt, where I spoke a few brief words of closure. Joe's family walked away, tearfully. The funeral director also exited temporarily; there was an unplanned gap in time, and I found myself alone with the casket.

"Well, goodbye, old crooner," I said to the box, and turned away to move on to my next responsibility. And then, from behind me, and making its way across the bronze plaques and nameplates of the hallway vaults, came an unmistakable refrain, sung in a muffled, yet familiar voice.

GA-ry, Indi-A-na,
GA-ry, Indi-A-na,
My home sweet home!

I did not look back. I could not. But even as the ephemeral lyric crawled across my skin and tugged at my breath, I only felt happy and reassured. It was a most agreeable mixture of music and memory that I only hoped was also being conveyed to Dr. Joseph Tallisman's family.

A Healing Silence

There is a great stillness that pervades the cemeteries, mausoleums, and memorial chapels that dot this otherwise noisy, boisterous, mercantile, and digitalized nation. We must grieve, we must process our anguish, and we must proceed with our lives in due time after losing someone because we simply are not going to see them in this life ever again. Yet I do maintain—from both my personal experience and the thoughtful reports of others—that we can hear from the dead.

It is sometimes hard *not* to hear from them; they are always part of one's subconscious and conscious thoughts and reveries. I've heard many times from people who tell me that "I heard from my father and he told me what to do"; or, "I didn't know how to deal with this issue but then I remembered something my mother once told me." It doesn't require a "psychic medium" or even an actual visitation. If you lean into your grief and remember your dead with courage and forthrightness, they will reward you with information and insight. Here, on this corporeal side, only a healthy soul that tackles bereavement with vulnerability and openness has a chance to learn something from a soul on the ethereal (other) side.

Part of the perplexity of our mortality is that regardless of science, beyond skepticism, we have no way to empirically prove there is not another dimension to our lives in this cosmos. And I am not speaking of absurd American sensations such as "Elvis sightings" or the preposterous manipulations of a séance, replete with the prescribed oval table, a specific setting of candles, and the number of people present divisible by three. Remembrance and tribute represent a dignified category of interaction with the dead; contrived trysts with celebrity dead or someone's own dear ones represent something else altogether and frequently amount to a series of burlesque mummeries. These have nothing to do with genuine, cleansing grief.

Better that the dead should come to us than that we should pursue them. It is usually more illuminating that way, less forced, and less incendiary. How many crimes have been committed by perpetrators—history is filled with "messiahs"—who rationalized their misdeeds based on messages or directives supposedly coerced from spirits or derived from their own narcissism. When we go after the dead, the living are often hurt. When the dead drift to us—at the cemetery, in church, or in any prayerful moment—the living are sometimes enlightened.

We can learn something from the dead if we find them in our dreams or discover them through the soft vestibule of our personal spirituality. A quiet visit at someone's grave or at the site of an urn can also create understanding and healing. There is nothing wrong or misguided about talking with a loved one at the site of his or her memorial marker; there are often important things to bestow and receive.

I don't think people should linger on and on with their dead, and I certainly affirm that we must accept mortality as the measure of life's limits. But I do not disclaim that we can detect some things from the dead, even as I saw a young girl's soul fly away from her body and heard a mausoleum rendition of a stanza of *The Music Man*.

Chapter Eight

Moving Forward:
How Does Grief Grow Us?

. . . .

"The hour of departure has arrived and we go our ways; I to die, and you to live. Which is better? Only God knows."
Socrates

In his book, *A Question of Character,* Thomas Reeves wrote the following about John F. Kennedy: "Jack took the loss of his favorite sister terribly hard. For the next several years, haunted by Kick's death[29] and fears about his physical condition, Jack spoke often about death. [One close friend] thought him 'deeply preoccupied by death' and later recalled a fishing trip in which Jack pondered the best ways to die."[30]

Reeves reported in his book that following his sister's tragic demise, the future president matured as a human being. His veneer of impossibly good looks and detached political charisma evolved into a more solemn view of life and providence. Reeves wrote: "Some of his male friends thought that Jack's new view of his mortality made him more companionable and interesting."

29 Kathleen "Kick" Kennedy died in a plane crash in France in 1948.
30 Thomas Reeves, *A Question of Character: A Life of John F. Kennedy* (New York: Prima Lifestyles, 1992).

There is no question about it. An unknown philosopher left us with these words: "Life asked Death, 'Why do people love me but hate you?' Death responded, 'Because you are a beautiful lie and I am a painful truth.'" Once we have confronted mortality and grieved, we are endowed with layers of heightened sensitivity, deeper empathy, and bittersweet wisdom. The "painful truth" transforms life from blissful simplicity into informed complexity. When I am in pain, I prefer to talk with somebody who has actually been tested by crisis rather than an unproved speechmaker who speaks gratuitously about matters he or she has not endured. The dead are the silent mentors of life-wisdom. If you or I are going to tell anyone, "I know how you feel," it cannot be an abstract declaration. It only rings true if it comes from hard-won experience. People who offer platitudes to us when we are in mourning usually mean well. People who speak to us after having actually suffered talk from hard experience.

"Grief is a teacher, when it sends us back to serve the living." When we embrace our sorrow and convert the anguish into genuine reflection, we can find out who we are and what values live within us. And then, if we are inspired to righteous deeds, there is a genuine transformation that turns pain into wisdom and mindfulness.

Such a transformation was realized by Robert F. Kennedy, the brother of President Kennedy. I described his personal change in a previous book called *Dangerous Friendship*.[31] For so long an inflexible, sometimes callous man driven by family ambition and fanatic loyalty to JFK, Bobby Kennedy was profoundly changed by his searing grief after the murder of his brother in Dallas on November 22, 1963.

After the shocking assassination of the young president, something began to happen within the shattered soul and the slight body of Bobby Kennedy. A number of his intimates have spoken or written about the

---

31 Ben Kamin, *Dangerous Friendship: Stanley Levison, Martin Luther King Jr., and the Kennedy Brothers* (Lansing: Michigan State University Press, 2014).

discernible change in the inconsolable man; grief softened Kennedy's hard soul and rigid sensibilities. Running a short-lived presidential campaign in 1968 (he was assassinated on June 5, moments after winning the California primary), Kennedy captured the imaginations and hopes of the nation's poor and underprivileged. He became a passionate advocate for African Americans, many of whom actually saw him as the ethical successor to Martin Luther King Jr., who had been gunned down just two months prior. Kennedy also developed a keen sense of outrage about the historic plight of Native Americans; in short, the calamity of his brother's death turned him into an unambiguously compassionate person and a visionary champion of human rights in America.

The iconic singer and civil rights leader Harry Belafonte, who had encouraged Bobby to seek the presidency, wrote that "Bobby had been transformed . . . the days of wondering how we might find access to his moral center were long gone."[32]

From *Dangerous Friendship*:
> Many historians have expounded upon the deepening of Robert Kennedy that occurred after he lost his brother. There are innumerable accounts of his midnight jaunts over the fence at Arlington National Cemetery, where he would spend hours in prayer over the president's grave. The eternal flame would capture the unspeakable woe etched permanently into the gaunt face, tears poured out of his eyes, and even his thick, wavy shock of hair would appear wracked and hopeless. He was known to disappear on solitary walks through Washington at all hours of the day or night; he donned his late brother's jackets and cufflinks and even transferred his papers into one of John's favored carry cases. [33]

32 Harry Belafonte, *My Song: A Memoir* (New York: Knopf, 2011) p. 337.
33 Ben Kamin, *Dangerous Friendship: Stanley Levison, Martin Luther King Jr., and the Kennedy Brothers* (Lansing: Michigan State University Press, 2014), p. 191–92.

Out of this well of bereavement came a rehabilitated soul. The scion of privilege and power, a patrician who had never really taken a strong interest in matters of social justice and human welfare, Robert F. Kennedy emerged from tragedy as a prophet of righteousness.

Kennedy did not appear to know how to deal with his grief; rather, it appeared the grief knew how to deal with him. It remade him into an uncommonly sympathetic and sensitive human being. That is why Kennedy was able to stand upon the back of a flatbed truck in Indianapolis on the night of April 4, 1968, and—in an impromptu speech—tell a crowd of primarily African Americans that Martin Luther King Jr. had just been murdered in Memphis. By his words and actions embracing social justice, he had *earned* the right to tell the stricken crowd:

> For those of you who are black and are tempted to be
> filled with hatred and distrust at the injustice of such
> an act, against all white people, I can only say that I can
> also feel in my own heart the same kind of feeling. I had
> a member of my family killed, but he was killed by a
> white man.[34]

Again and again, in my own experience and in the study of historical men and women, I hear the echo of the prayer book: "Grief is a great teacher, when it sends us back to serve the living."

Reuben's Challenge

I once watched a man die over the course of two long and grueling years.

In the mid-1980s, I began work at a large and historic synagogue in the Midwest, serving as associate rabbi to a distinguished cleric whom I will call Reuben Cohen. We were rather dissimilar in style and personality; Reuben was a prominent theological scholar and retained an almost grim formality. He was an aloof man of erudite habits who

34 "April 4, 1968: How RFK saved Indianapolis," *Indianapolis Star*, April 2, 2015.

kept some distance from others and who himself admitted he was more suited to academia than to spiritual leadership. In fact, his father, an extremely eminent sage and leader of this same congregation, had anointed Reuben as his successor. Reuben simply inherited the position without any professional or contractual lobbying.

As it turned out, he and I became good working partners and genuinely liked one another. There was a successful symmetry: I enjoyed mixing with people and working with youngsters; Reuben was content to withdraw, read and reflect in his study, have lunch with the wealthy patrons of the temple, and deliver his weekly sermon to a crowd of mostly elderly people.

I had been in the community about two years. Reuben was fifty-nine, tall and bulky, an exquisitely handsome man with a strong jaw and a Princeton pedigree. He had suffered a severe bout of pneumonia while traveling in South Africa that turned out to be foreboding. As he began to visibly weaken and deteriorate, his face recessed and his strong shoulders sagged. The diagnosis finally became public—he was stricken with a merciless brain lymphoma. I kept thinking how dreadfully ironic that a man of such a superior mind and intellect be afflicted in the brain.

As I began to fill in more and more for him, my relationship with Reuben and his family also plummeted. After about a year of this situation, and as the synagogue leadership began to accede to the terminal truth about their leader, I came to be viewed as Reuben's successor. This was not an enviable state of affairs—most especially for Reuben, who fought heroically for two years against the disease before finally succumbing to it.

He continued to work and to appear at synagogue events until about six months before his demise. He was not always lucid. He sometimes collapsed on the podium. On one occasion, when his cranial issues caused him to completely go blank as he was trying to read from the prayer book in front of a Sabbath congregation, I walked over from my pulpit seat to assist him. He looked at me, his left eye drooping from the cancer, and struck me on the shoulder with his fist.

I had to covertly shadow him at weddings and funerals at various sites and venues in order to step in when he literally was unable to function and perform. He was as stubborn as he was brave. His refusal to surrender certainly prolonged his much-too-short life. Sadly, some people began to prefer he not appear at their milestone events; some even came to resent his obstinacy because they didn't want a spectacle interfering with their ceremony or occasion.

But as time went on, and before Reuben became too unwell to continue appearing in public on any regular basis, there was a discernible change in his personality and behavior. A previously unknown sympathetic strain began to possess him. He noticed the children of our religious school and smiled at them, frequently putting his hands on their heads as they rushed by. He was more warmly present—and woefully congenial—in the room with his congregants. He sought out other staff members for lunch outings or just conversational interludes. He looked forward to being taken out to the movies in the evenings; the senior staff rotated in this tender responsibility.

As his own grief enveloped him, he allowed himself to be vulnerable. The distance between him and others noticeably lessened. I saw fear and loneliness in the eyes of this once-towering figure who, despite his horrific illness, managed to write a brilliant book (hardly his first) about the origins of scripture that was published posthumously. I noted with awe and admiration that the author picture he had approved for the book jacket was not his long-standing, gleaming photo of the good-looking young man with a thick head of hair, sturdy facial features, and piercing eyes that radiated both hardiness and wisdom; rather, it was the authentic image of Reuben as he looked during his end of days—pale, wracked, lightless eyes, a hurting, lusterless smile, yet a man replete with tenacious dignity.

On one early afternoon, he had invited me to lunch at a plush downtown restaurant. There was precariousness between us. Reuben was cogent that day, in between the daunting and draining chemotherapy and radiation treatments, the relentless indignity of his cruel malady, the undeniable fright that surely filled him every waking moment. He spoke to me quietly and with poise. He was uncharacteristically forthright and humble.

"Look, we probably should talk. I don't know how much life I have left."

"I am deeply concerned about you, Reuben," I replied. "And I just want to be helpful." It was clear to me that he was struggling very hard to come to terms with his own woe and fears.

He spoke up again. "It took me so damn long to even walk through this restaurant. I'm an old man." He was only sixty, and still had a measure of the hulk that had carried him on the Princeton football team.

"No, you're not an old man," I said. "Old men quit." Reuben smiled and thanked me. He seemed touched—maybe even lifted—by the remark. He dug into his plate and we continued to eat for a few moments. I finally said, "What do you wish to talk about, Reuben?"

"I don't really know," he said, without edginess. But then suddenly, his face turned stormy and his tone shifted. He stared at me intensely and blared out, "You know, you're just like the rest of them. The rest of you young rabbis. You came here to upgrade from your previous position. You'll move on after a while and advance to your own congregation, using what you did here as your laurels. You're all the same."

I understood he was sick, but I had too much respect for him not to take up his challenge. "Wait a minute, Reuben. You can't talk to me like that. You never applied for a job in your life like I had to apply and earn the position I hold. You got the job because your father passed it along to you. I had to *earn* it from you while going up against a bunch of other candidates. You've never even had to draw up a résumé. How can you come at me for just doing what I had to do like everyone else?"

My boss looked at me while slowly chewing on his sea bass. He nodded his head and issued a barely audible "Hmm." He didn't say much of anything else until we walked out of the restaurant together, exchanging pleasantries. But I know that he did not feel like a dying person for that interlude. He just felt like a person. He walked away, smiling.

Money or Memories?

On May 1, 2015, forty-seven-year-old David Goldberg died suddenly and unexpectedly. He collapsed off an exercise machine and split his head open on the floor. It was later determined that he had suffered a cardiac arrhythmia, which led to the devastating fall. Goldberg was the husband of Facebook COO Sheryl Sandberg, mentioned earlier. Sandberg, who had led a relatively gilded life up to this tragedy, was overwhelmed and, in her own words, engulfed by "the deep loneliness of my loss."[35] As one journalist expressed, "Grief nearly crushed her, and she wasn't afraid to say that out loud."[36]

It's important to remember that, at the core, Sheryl Sandberg, a talented and skilled corporate groundbreaker, is nonetheless a young mother who was mercilessly widowed. Individuals with the kind of power and affluence she enjoys sometimes have difficulty with problems and challenges they can't buy out. Sadly, over the years, I have often observed people of privilege who never really had any major personal issues to contend with become completely unhinged when struck by a

---

35 Sheryl Sandberg and Adam Grant, *Option B: Facing Adversity, Building Resilience, and Finding Joy.* Copyright © 2017 by OptionB.Org.

36 This quote and other information in this section is largely derived from "Can a Super-Rich Jewish Woman from Silicon Valley Help Americans Learn to Grieve?" The article, by Jane Eisner, appeared in the May 19, 2017 edition of the *Forward,* of which Eisner is editor-in-chief.

serious illness or a tragic event in their lives. They lash out in frustrated terror and fail to achieve an outlet for their vexations.

No portfolio, no level of clout or prominence, changes the core being of a mother and wife—most grievously when she is widowed. And especially when she is young and with small children. Sheryl Sandberg found herself walking a grim, unfamiliar, and unwanted road; her celebrity was no veil for her anguish. She has described the brutality of watching her children collapse at their father's grave, "I didn't know what to do. It was one of the worst moments of my life. I wasn't rational. I wanted to help. I wanted to comfort."

Making good use of her considerable means and connections, Sandberg called upon a number of grief scholars and therapists to help her analyze—and share—her bereavement and recovery. The result was her book and seminar series called *Option B*. As she applied herself, the grief grew Sandberg from helplessness to helpfulness. The book drew from a profoundly raw and tender Facebook post about her mourning that immediately "went viral." As journalist Jane Eisner wrote in 2017, "It became a remarkable social phenomenon, shared more than 400,000 times and positioning Sandberg as unusually vulnerable and as honest, helpful, and kind." Eisner added, with words that reflect some of the themes I discussed earlier:

> She was already writing that optimistic bromides don't help someone whose world has been shattered, that mourners don't need to be told life will get better when they can't believe it will, that instead they need their pain to be acknowledged and the uncertainty in their future legitimated. Ask not, "How are you?" Ask instead, "How are you *today*?"[37]

Sandberg focused on this issue, with notable empathy for the freshly grieved, in her book:

---

37 From the previously footnoted *Forward* article by Jane Eisner.

Many people who had not experienced loss, even some very close friends, didn't know what to say to me or my kids. Their discomfort was palpable, especially in contrast to our previous ease. As the elephant in the room went unacknowledged, it started acting up, trampling over my relationships . . . Friends were asking, "How are you?" but I took this as more of a standard greeting than a genuine question. I wanted to scream back, "My husband just died, how do you think I am?" I didn't know how to respond to pleasantries. Aside from that, *how was the play, Mrs. Lincoln?*[38]

To her credit, Sandberg forcefully converted her anguish into wisdom and with much-needed direction for millions of her readers and followers. As already intimated here, this isn't always the case when advantaged people endure grief or terminal illness. This is hardly their fault or intent. Exactly because life hasn't tested them before, they are sometimes unable to deal with a problem of such overwhelming gravity and consequence.

I once visited the billionaire owner of an insurance conglomerate who was hospitalized with an incurable ailment. Surrounded by dutiful assistants and a host of entertainment gadgets and infused with pain medications, he dismissed his entourage when I arrived. I thought we were about to have an evocative discussion about his situation. He looked at me and impatiently blurted, "Rabbi, do you know how to operate a goddam VCR? I've got this movie I want to see and it just won't go in!"

I spent the next twenty minutes fiddling with the tape, trying to jam it into the machine until it finally caught. Meanwhile, he was placing irritable phone calls to colleagues and subordinates while I, on my knees in my suit, struggled with his valuable copy of *Raiders of the Lost Ark*. I

---

38 From *Option B*, by Sheryl Sandberg and Adam Grant.

got up and announced to him, "Okay, it's fixed." He responded, "Okay, thanks for stopping by, Rabbi." And then he dismissed me with a nod of his head.

I thought about that hollow moment—and the lost opportunity— when I conducted his burial four months later. He had died restlessly and with tremendous anger. I so wished to have helped him with more than an adjustment of his VCR unit. Alas, he did not grow from his grief. He just died and left behind a lot of money for his family but not many memories.

Grief and Its Legacy

My own mother certainly didn't grow from the grief of losing my father. Granted, it was sudden and shocking, and my parents were only in their forties at the time. The thing I recall most vividly in the days following the calamity was my mother regularly scurrying into the kitchen and, regardless of who was nearby, flailing herself against the sink and then vomiting into it. It was hard to watch, and we did try with all our might to comfort her. And even though I was twenty-three, my younger brother and sister and me were nonetheless just newly fatherless children and were fraught with our own terrors.

My mom and dad had been grade school sweethearts and—in spite of their frequent outbursts of yelling and contending—she had worshipped him. They had traveled a long road together as immigrants to the United States. Both were young war veterans from another land; together they negotiated many social, professional, and financial uncertainties and ethnic pressures. I recall with pride that they bore with dignity and resilience the steady flow of xenophobic ugliness that accrued for them in the new and bewildering provinces of Colorado and Ohio in the 1950s and 1960s. My grief for them does not preclude my admiration and respect for the cultural hardships with which they contended; on the contrary, there is a kinship with them that is stirred through my sorrow.

Like many people, they were haunted by unfulfilled dreams. Both had struggled in their respective fields (he was a scientific engineer; she was a schoolteacher). There were setbacks and even humiliations for both of them, jobwise. Both were headstrong, sometimes shrill, and they didn't consult clinical therapists.

When my father died, my mother felt cheated, abandoned, and angry. Predictably, she did not seek out professional help. Rather, she sought out her three children in order to transfer her rage and the blame for the loss. Her own torment completely untreated and unhandled, she wreaked spiritual havoc on us. She had always been something of a manipulator who routinely played favorites with her kids, generally pitting one against the other. She leaned toward sulkiness. But now, weighed down by an indescribable and unquestionably unfair blow, her behavior became both extreme and histrionic.

She resented me for being married already and trying to build a new life. She begrudged my younger brother much tenderness simply because he physically resembled our father. She imprisoned our little sister—who was only twelve—with possessiveness, the emotional responsibility for Mom's healing, with the burden of her tragic secrets, and with inappropriate confidences about men she might date in the aftermath of losing her husband. My mother would often foist the question to my sister about a prospective courter, "What do you think, should I let him stay over?" My little sister was but a preteen at the time. She was essentially robbed of a normal adolescence.

I did not know what to say to my mother, given her inconsolable heaves and breathtaking mood swings. We butted heads and hearts—though I knew then and I still lament her despondent existence in the prison of herself. Although she was often very funny, a skilled and colorful storyteller, loved to sing, could be extremely charming, and was a gifted and energetic teacher for other people's children, she unfortunately trafficked in demons in the presence of her own kids.

Surely, some of her ordeal was fueled by guilt. The night he would die, my father left the house after another screaming bout with my mother and hulked off to the handball court where he would drop dead. They never said goodbye to each other nor even patched the argument. Their final words to each other were inflamed with fury. There can't be any question that this tore at my mother's soul for the remainder of her days. Grief, like a dark eagle, swoops in on those kinds of human scraps. My father never knew the serenity of old age; my mother's face remained a shadow until she finally died from heart ailments, diabetes, and dementia at the age of eighty-one.

I still wonder: did my mother not see my father's death coming? Should she not have reached out to him in his own suffering and turmoil? When I attempted to ask her about this later, she rebuffed me, circumvented the subject, and reminded me of how I was too busy with my graduate schoolwork and my marriage to devote her proper attention. Grief was controlling her most detrimentally and I wish now, over forty years later, that I had been more dynamic and directive in getting her to a capable bereavement therapist or at least a support group of some kind. That is what any one of us should do when we see a person upon whom grief has inflicted such damaging dysfunction. Having failed to intervene more forcefully and positively so long ago has extended and complicated my grief for both my parents beyond any normal limits. We should not concede to death more than it has already taken. Grief needs to have a life of its own but it should also inform our own life. If grief doesn't teach you anything about living, then all you have from it is the dying.

As for me, I saw my father's death coming in my dreams and my daytime reflections. I observed his frequent gloominess, his erratic changes of spirits, and his white-hot explosions of bile. I surreptitiously read in his journals that he actually could see himself lying in a coffin at Cincinnati's Weil Funeral Home—a dark prophecy fulfilled. I knew something that was like a stone in my soul: my father, given to bursts of sentiment, short on patience, could never find a place to alight.

Wise friends and colleagues counseled me to embrace these apprehensions. (Of course, I was fortunate enough to have access to such people; not everyone does.) I came to bear his intermittent announcements, "Don't make me into a grandfather!" I did not enjoy such declarations but grew from understanding that it was a function of his own despairs, a failing marriage, and his developing war with aging. He got his wish about not being a grandfather; I hold my granddaughters now, a generation later and a generation wiser. It is okay if we discover that we learned about how *not* to do things from departed parents or other elders. They were still our parents and they gave us life. They were usually doing the best they could or were simply trapped in their personalities.

I fervently reject the Judeo-Christian notion that the sins of the parents are visited upon the children. That is an untenable proposition. Grief is hard enough without laying on the burdens of guilt-by-association or any other religiously bent distractions. That is why I assert in this book that the answer to how we grieve is a therapeutic blend of personal history, applicable rituals that make sense to each of us, and the thoughtful, circumspect support of family and friends.

On the other hand, I find tremendous discernment in the Fourth Commandment inscribed in the Hebrew Scripture. "Honor thy father and mother." Brilliant that it doesn't read, "*Love* thy father and mother." Love cannot be commanded or legislated. Nor does every parent who ever lived deserve to be loved. Most parents do well; some do very poorly with damaging, demoralizing effects. They sometimes broke our hearts in the way they treated us, overlooked us, or even emotionally maimed us. Our grief is muddied by the fact that we are ambivalent about our feelings, which often bring on even more guiltiness and uncertainty. But not every person can be revered. Love is an earned condition. However, to *honor* the fact of someone's parenthood is a reasonable and edifying requirement. No matter what, when we honor our parents' memory, we emerge better acquainted with our origins and, as necessary, the liabilities that come with them. If some parents don't earn love, they nonetheless deserve a legacy. If you have a spot on your arm, it is still your arm with which you reach out to others.

In the American bereavement culture, we are reticent to just tell the truth when it comes to remembering and eulogizing complicated people. That doesn't mean we should get up at a funeral and lambast or excoriate a departed person who angered or bedeviled us. There are certain protocols of dignity and restraint that come with the territory. Difficult people must be honored because they were human beings, even if they were flawed. But to heap unqualified praise on a person who really wasn't entirely praiseworthy is to create a fiction. Fiction and grief are not redeeming partners. It is also not therapeutically supportive to pretend that someone was one way when he or she simply was not. *Remember them as they were and respect their existence.* And if you can't love them, honor them. Cherish the good; learn from the bad. They've already paid for it with their lives.

Grief and Relief

What happens if one feels relief after a good person dies?

One of the more bewildering challenges people face occurs when they discover such unexpected latent feelings in mourning. People are often very hard on themselves about this natural and appropriate sensation; it is a normal response in certain instances. Sometimes, a person—even a most cherished individual—just *needs* to go. And you have to let him or her go. Perhaps it's an impossibly ill or tormented spouse or parent. Maybe even a child of yours—if you feel a certain sense of reprieve when a tortured soul or a diseased body leaves this world, well, that does not mean you did not love that person. It is okay to realize that with death, nothing more can happen to a person you love. It is okay to feel some exoneration when the journey was hard and long.

I used to observe a strong-limbed elderly couple walking briskly together, hand-in-hand, many evenings in the wooded and verdant Shaker Heights, Ohio. Even a brisk autumn wind did not deter them from their regular constitutional. I knew the long-married man and woman, a physician and professor respectively, had recently lost a son who was in his early forties. The son had not been stricken with any particular physical illness. He simply never learned to adjust to life in this world and, with his various social afflictions and behavioral disorders, had inadvertently caused his family tremendous and unyielding distress. He was in out and of behavioral health institutes, recovery clinics, and, not infrequently, city jail cells.

As much as he emotionally punished his parents with his demons, that is how much they loved him. But there was simply no resolution for the young man's malaise—not even medication healed his soul.

I met them along the path one night. They were congregants of mine, and I knew them well enough to talk about personal things. I inquired about their situation and expressed my concern and condolences. They had not been in touch with the synagogue or me when their son died. They were kindly and gracious that evening yet, at the same time, seemed a bit self-conscious, perhaps due to my position in the community. They were embarrassed because it might have appeared (to them) that they were not properly bewailing their lost son. "Not at all," I assured them. And then I asked, "What makes you feel that way?"

They looked at each other. Then the mother spoke, "Charlie was a hard person to help. He was that way from when he was a child. So much anger and suffering in that poor boy. There was never a moment of peace or certainty. We were tired, very tired when he died, Rabbi. We did our best; but it was actually a relief when he finally found peace."

I listened and felt admiration for these brave parents. Before I could say anything, the father asked, his voice cracking just a bit, "Are we bad people, Rabbi?"

"Of course not. You appear to be two very good people who should keep on walking."

. . . .

Jimmy Rosen had been an active and heralded pediatric surgeon for well over fifty years and performed some seventeen thousand operations on infants and youngsters. He saved or extended countless young lives. Tall, burly, and ruggedly handsome at ninety-one years of age, he told me his life story during weekly visits for about a year in 2016 and 2017. He and his wife Joy had shared in the birth of four children, with three of them being success stories and delivering much comfort and elation to both parents. Almost a year into our association, however, Jimmy suddenly opened up about his middle son, Daniel. "Danny was a difficult son to have and he knew how to press my buttons." I was a bit surprised, having met the other adult children and their families. It was a winning generation of thriving professionals, standouts in the arts, medicine, and social services. Jimmy had done nothing but rave about his children and grandchildren for months. Now we came to a crack in the earth.

"Danny went to a Quaker college, which I thought was ideal," Jimmy related. Unfortunately, the school was saturated with drug dealers and users. "He succumbed," the heavy-shouldered father told me. His son became addicted to "marijuana, cocaine, and God-knows-what." Slumping a bit, the proud man said, "Joy and I hardly even ever take an aspirin, so to have Danny become a drug addict was a big problem for us."

Danny went through several jobs and a number of relationships. His parents held on to the hope that he'd find "a nice young woman" and settle down with some measure of stability and happiness. Instead, Danny died, alone, in a motel room after a massive coronary.

"Danny was always treated like an outsider," Jimmy lamented. "In school, if the guys were throwing the ball around, they wouldn't include him, or they would just throw the ball at his head. Later, the drugs and the self-medication just caught up with him."

Jimmy told me that his wife Joy was "broken up, more than I because, through the years, Danny and I had a relationship that was difficult for me. He would be somewhere and he would call me and say he didn't have any money and I'd send him some money. The other kids would tell me that was the most foolish thing to do because he's going to use it to buy drugs. The truth is that Danny would always find tasks to do that would make his life easier and mine more difficult. But I went along with it and tried to make things for him as easy as possible."

I asked Jimmy what has helped him to maintain his strength after the loss of his son.

"I must admit," replied the father, "that I had the attitude at least that's the end of a problem that had been absolutely plaguing us for all the years Danny was around. I wasn't happy about my reaction but I thought it was realistic. His mother could not stop crying, and I understand that. But I didn't quite feel the way she did. Because Danny fought with other family members and he was always cantankerous. He was hard to be with and difficult to care for. Needless to say, we did the best we could. I felt relieved, frankly."

Jimmy had no apologies, only sadness. "I tell you I welcomed Danny's birth as if he was a little messiah. He was the boy I always wanted. But it didn't turn out that way." Then Jimmy wiped tears out of his eyes with his thick and weathered fingers and it was clear that he simply had no more words and would not give to his grief any more than it had already taken.

So what is grief, if not the most painfully informative experience we humans come to know? It is also a chance to visit with somebody who is gone from this world. We offer the best homage to our dead when we apply the truth to our visits—just as we tried to do when they were on this side.

Chapter Nine

Faith and Hope: Because Every Soul Takes Its Own Journey

. . . .

"Faith is to believe what you do not see; the reward
of this faith is to see what you believe."
Saint Augustine

Grief is as personal a bridge crossing as it is a necessary passage. This was especially evident to me one day when I visited two different people in the hospital within an hour of each other.

The first patient, Mr. Englander, was a normally hardy gentleman, exceptionally fit, in his mid-seventies. Though I had never grown close to Mr. Englander, who was given to brusqueness, I admired his vitality and feistiness. In business, he got things done; on the golf course, he reveled.

Today, however, Mr. Englander was not reveling. He was grieving, though not for someone who had died. He was grieving for himself. He was in a well-appointed hospital room, laid up with an ankle he'd broken on the fairway. He had lost his footing on what should have been a pristine surface, interrupting his game, his mood, and evidently his entire existence. Mr. Englander was in mournful, heated spirits.

"Are you going to tell me that this is what God wants?" he growled. "Is this something I am supposed to learn from?" He would have no part in accepting his predicament or putting it into perspective.

"I just wanted to say hello," I offered, wondering how a man with an adoring and healthy wife, three successful children, several grandchildren, three imported luxury cars, two homes, and several sets of personalized golf clubs could turn a broken ankle into a theological stalemate. Mr. Englander flinched a bit and I did recognize that he was in some pain. He said, "Well, that's fine. Thank you for coming. But look, this is just unfair. It is just plain cruel. What am I supposed to do now?"

He railed about the injustice of the situation. Why was God testing him in this way? He would probably be unable to play in the upcoming tournament at his Florida condominium complex. While the man was in genuine physical discomfort, his anger about this inconvenience to his social and business calendars was beyond repair. He was inconsolable, in spite of the many gifts of his life.

Now his wife entered the room, along with two of his grandchildren. They smiled shyly at him, getting a tad more warmth in return than I had received, but not much. Clearly his family had long ago learned to submit to Mr. Englander's dominant acidity and sense of entitlement. The entire circle was ill-equipped to deal with the notion of limitations and this, sadly, would hamper their ability to grieve in the near future.

I excused myself and left the Englander family. I then went to visit an elderly woman who lay alone in her room, several floors below and in much more modest quarters. Following the peevish Mr. Englander, I dreaded what I might encounter from Mrs. Dworkin, a woman with real problems.

Mrs. Dworkin had been immobilized and bedridden for four months. A deterioration of her spinal cord had effectively ended her active life. I understood there was no hope for her to ever walk or even stand up again. As I entered the room, she raised her eyes at me and smiled. I recall thinking that I had never seen such a beneficent face. She smiled and absolutely reached out to me with her countenance.

Though she was completely still, I felt as though she had wrapped her arms around me.

The woman then proceeded to tell me about her great and good fortune. "Do you know how lucky I am, Rabbi?" She repeatedly asked me this startling question. And she exclaimed, "I have my children who love me and my beautiful grandchildren who sing to me and write me lovely poems. The doctors are marvelous here and the care is so good. I have a wonderful life. I know I can't move, but I am lucky to be alive and to know the people who make my life worth living."

It goes without saying that I benefited from visiting this remarkable grandmother who was in the closing stages of her life but was not closing her heart. I was inspired by her, and remain so to this day. Mrs. Dworkin did not query me about why God or the fates had done this to her. She said that she had her faith to fall back upon. "It gives me strength and encouragement." Mrs. Dworkin was then quiet for a moment. I saw in her face that she was struggling with a lot of distress yet remaining in a good place about her situation.

"What are you thinking about?" I asked her.

"I just prayed a little. I prayed that my family will be okay when I die from all of this. I don't want my family to feel bad for me. Of course, I want to be missed by them. But I'm okay with dying. I've been given the time now to realize how much there's been to my life."

Mrs. Dworkin was unknowingly giving me life lessons that are useful partners to the process of grief. Hearing her celebrate her inner strength and her accord with mortality, I actually felt ashamed for all the times I lumped small nuisances, petty annoyances, and minor distractions all together as "the problems of life." Why do we get stuck on minor things that matter so little on the journey? Why do we bristle and even yell at salespeople when we are miffed about a purchase? People come into a mobile phone store and go ballistic over this or that app on their device. *It's just a phone, for goodness' sake!* Why do we get entangled in all these silly rivalries over wealth and position and status? Why do we Americans so heavily evaluate one another over the kind of cars we drive?

Why does all this kind of stuff even matter when life is so fleeting and brief? Grief hits hard but it hits even harder if one hasn't learned to grieve from confronting all limitations and conclusions. Divorce is grief; being fired is mourning; coping with disease is bereavement; discovering that one's child is addicted to opioids is suffering. Enduring these difficulties along life's path is so hard yet these moments can spiritually mentor us for the ultimate woe of someone's death—or even for our own.

Grief, a dark angel of renewal, comes to distill all the banalities. Though she was already an astute person before contracting a spinal malady, Mrs. Dworkin recognized what's most important at the most dangerous time in her life. As I lingered with her, I suddenly felt a wave of heavy sympathy for the prickly Mr. Englander, who fidgeted impatiently in his bed a few flights up. While I'd never have wanted him to suffer, I did wish that he had somehow garnered the therapy of suffering. I wish he had been tested in ways that grew and softened him.

When Mr. Englander became terminally ill a year later with lymphoma, he was completely unequipped for the situation. Lashing out at his family and his employees, he refused to relinquish control of his business affairs. He doggedly maintained his lifelong secretiveness about personal matters. Live alone; die alone.

His children were left with a significant lack of input with respect to the family enterprise. It's not that Mr. Englander did not know what to tell his children; it's that he would *not* tell them. Clouding the atmosphere, complicating the grief, restricting the closure, Mr. Englander's unwillingness to acknowledge life's limits made his final few months on earth a desolate passage from material wealth into spiritual oblivion. His oldest son came to me and said, "I don't know how to grieve for my father." I just listened, but thought to myself, *Your father didn't know how to live for his children.*

I sat by Mr. Englander's side during the final weeks of his illness. He was not talkative. I watched as he used his right hand to press on the bedside device that delivered morphine into his bloodstream. *What a lonely hand*, I thought. So many palms pressed in elaborate deals yet so few occasions when the hand had actually touched anybody. I should have offered Mr. Englander a firm homily on priorities a year earlier when the grumpy retailer lay in bed with only his broken ankle and a missed golf outing. And yet, who was I to presume his way of dealing with things? Every soul takes its own journey. Our duty is to grieve for them, not to judge them.

I went over to the nursing home where Mrs. Dworkin had since transferred. She was making a little progress with her spine and was now able to turn her head a bit. I told her about Mr. Englander, that his situation was grave, and maybe I should have been more of a support for him when he was still healthy. She smiled with understanding and asked me:

"Did he learn anything when he broke his ankle playing golf?"

"No, not really," I answered.

"So what could he learn from cancer?"

. . . .

Through my work over the years, and certainly in writing this book, I have been asking myself why we Americans are so reticent about lamenting our dead. Why do we permit the media and retail cultures to desensitize us to the necessary therapy of authentic, personal grief? Why do we sometimes defer the hard sorrow required to channel our loss in favor of banalities and theatrics at funeral services? Why do well-meaning people and hyperactive clergy sometimes avoid talking directly about the real person who died (substituting hollow anecdotes or tiresome preachments that invoke gods more than people) when we want to visit with, think about, and recall *the human being who is now so missed?* So many of us don't know how to grieve because American social mores make us think we are supposed to entertain, feed, and reassure others exactly when we are in our own worst pain ever.

When we aré struggling with the question of how to grieve, one overriding answer is to immediately establish a relationship with all the realities that come with the grief:

a) This is dreadful and devastating; no amount of sweetening and aromatizing of the situation will offer any long-term results, and will actually skew the pain from eventual release.

b) Recall the departed as they lived; tell and reflect upon their life stories with sensitivity and love but not with embellishment or over-glorification. The dead are best recalled as they were and it keeps our grieving process therapeutic if we more or less stick with the truth.

I remember when my neighbor Bob died. Bob was, like me, the father of two high school girls. Before his illness began to slow him down, we would take many hearty walks under the shady oaks of our suburban Cleveland community. Bob, an African American, had a passionate interest in multicultural relations and social justice. Our children were close, and we all spent a lot of time at each other's homes. He retained his bravery and dignity while undergoing treatments for a savage kidney cancer. Three days after his death, I attended his funeral at a community church. Reflecting Bob's strong penchant for inclusiveness, the crowd was diverse in color and creed.

A number of family members and friends got up to speak. It was a small, modest, wooden sanctuary. The people were simple, hardworking folk. However, they said many things about Bob that were *pro forma*. He was kind, graceful, and good. He loved his faith. He was a perfect father to his children and a devoted husband. The well-intentioned reciters could have been a collective greeting card. We got no authentic histories of Bob: his values, his relationship with family, his professional career, his spiritual life, his flaws, his skills and strengths, his yearnings. Suddenly, a young man, twentyish, fit, stepped up to the lectern. He announced that he was Bob's nephew. He then proceeded to decry the cookie-cutter nature of the tributes.

"Our family certainly appreciates you all coming and hearing nice things about my uncle. But nobody is really saying anything about Uncle B himself. Even mentioning that he liked to be called Uncle B a lot. Even by his own kids sometimes. Remember that, Eve?" The nephew was pointing to his cousin, Bob's daughter.

Eve nodded, smiling, glimmering now with tears. "Yes, he just loved all of the kids calling him Uncle B. He liked being everybody's uncle, which was the way he was. Brought us those cheesy little gifts all the time! Socks and sports caps and all this candy we had to hide from our parents." A release of group laughter filled the room.

The nephew continued to speak extemporaneously. "Everybody who's been up here, I know you were just doing the right thing. But nobody really knows what to say. And I keep thinking that the only person, the one person, who'd know what to say is the person missing here today. Bob would have known what to say. About the things he cared about. About how much he loved watching baseball and taking his family to the ballpark. That he was a great scientist and chemical engineer and hated how we are destroying the environment. That he was a diehard patriot. What about how he adored jazz music and even listened to it when he was down or something. Can't anybody share something that will really help us remember Uncle B?"

Silence now filled the church. People rubbed their foreheads. Some were confused by the audacious orator. Some wiped away tears. Then, after a noticeable bit of rumbling in the back, an older gentleman, elderly, was walking up to the lectern. He was carrying a portable CD player with speakers. As the nephew gave way, the old man carefully set the machine upon the lectern. He cleared his throat and looked at us without any expression—but for love. He said, "I put together some of the music Bob liked. You know, when he git into one of those moods of his. Let me just play a few selections and we can think about old Bob."

In a moment, we heard a medley of artists, including Jack McDuff, Herb Ellis, and Cassandra Wilson delivering blues, guitar pieces, vocals, saxophone solos, and piano bits. People nodded, swayed, and sang along with the songs. There were intermittent sighs as each person there experienced a resonating moment of visiting with Bob—a certain lyric, a particular stanza, a defined beat, sent each one of us back to a living part of him. I saw Bob walking with me, as we both wiped our brows in the summer humidity, and he waxed intelligently and fervently about the inexcusable damage we humans were doing to the ozone layer. I listened to him describe and chuckle adoringly about his children's adolescent adventures. I heard his laughter. I relived his plunges into self-loathing. I saw his roundish, welcoming face, wizened by time, defeat, resiliency, and then the illness itself. The music revealed Bob to me and his soul filled the room and a piece of it landed within each one of us. We danced with Bob across the bridge and then let him go as himself.

It turns out that every soul takes its own journey and makes its own harmony. When grieving, listen for the unique melody of the one you miss so much. Honor lost lives by remembering how they sang to you. Pay tribute to them by pronouncing their names out loud and thus never denying them their singular identities in heaven and earth.

· · · · · · · · · · ·

Perhaps no one has ever declared publicly what he wanted for his own funeral and what his legacy should be more poignantly than Rev. Martin Luther King Jr. Just two months prior to his April 4, 1968, assassination in Memphis, King spoke to his congregation on February 4 at the Ebenezer Baptist Church in Atlanta. He was afflicted with a terrible dread of being killed throughout his thirteen years of stewarding the Civil Rights Movement and suffered from intermittent bouts of depression and deep fatigue. He was always apprehensive and fatalistic; he just knew his life would be ended by bullets. He released some of his angst and gave his directives in a sudden turn of subject at the end of his Sunday sermon on February 4.

> If any of you are around when I have to meet my day, I don't want a long funeral. And if you get somebody to deliver the eulogy, tell them not to talk too long. And every now and then I wonder what I want them to say. Tell them not to mention that I have a Nobel Peace Prize—that isn't important. Tell them not to mention that I have three or four hundred other awards—that's not important. Tell them not to mention where I went to school.
>
> I'd like somebody to mention that day that Martin Luther King Jr. tried to give his life serving others . . .
>
> But I just want to leave a committed life behind. And that's all I want to say.[39]

We all can't be so declarative about our memorial wishes. Not everyone has the loins to discuss such a subject while still here on this earth. Nor do most people have access to a podium that allows them to

---

39 *The King Papers Encyclopedia* of the Martin Luther King Jr. Research and Education Institute, Stanford University, Dr. Clayborne Carson, director. https://kinginstitute. stanford.edu.

ventilate and release some elegiac murmurs in a safe and comforting place, surrounded by followers and disciples.

But what can we do to emulate Dr. King's clarity of mind and his wish to gently guide his parish family for what he knew was inevitable? First, note King's humility: "I don't want a long funeral. And if you get somebody to deliver the eulogy, tell them not to talk too long." Note his ethical teaching: "I'd like somebody to mention that day that Martin Luther King Jr. tried to give his life serving others." King died with a modest estate, yet has he not endowed the world with an enormously precious moral treasury?

Then "bookmark" his precept that "all of the other shallow things will not matter." So if you are near the end of life and are still able to, then tell your family to skip over "the shallow things." If you are grieving, cherish the ideas and principles your loved one shared with you and taught you. I always ask people I serve in bereavement: "What did your father, mother, or other dear one teach you?" What people leave us monetarily does not distill our grief. It's what they *gave* us spiritually and emotionally that helps us to grieve with gratitude and purpose. Or find a way to honor their existences if they were harder than others to praise. Every soul takes its own journey. Nobody should be judging when we are grieving. We should be remembering.

Afterword

When Grief Became My Necessary Companion

· · · · · · · · · · ·

"How lucky am I to have something that
makes saying goodbye so hard."
A. A. Milne

W hen one day, panicking from the loneliness and grief, I donned
a bathing suit, t-shirt, and flip-flops, grabbed a towel and
walked down to the swimming pool of my complex, I knew I had hit
rock bottom. It was a grayish yet hot day and I was frantic to be around
people. *Anyone.* It didn't matter if I knew them or not. I wanted to hear
the sounds of voices, the sight of children around the water, splashing
and laughing, the cheerful good spirits of friendly strangers—*anything*.
I wanted an opportunity to just engage folks in repartee. I was so
desperately lonely and so trapped in the box of deferred sorrow that it
physically hurt my gut.

I reached the pool area, blinking in the heat. Emptiness: there
wasn't a single person there. The chlorinated water laughed at me with
ghoulish refrain. The empty chairs sneered at me. I almost fell to my
knees in sadness and fright. My heart was pounding with stress and
isolation. I dragged myself back up the hill to my apartment, the burden

of unfulfilled grief piercing me with hopelessness and downheartedness. I felt like I had fallen off the edge of the earth.

This was not an easy book to write. I began working on it during a clinical recovery period for myself—recovery from grief, both specific and accumulated. I traveled through it while recuperating from what was diagnosed as depression. A then-recent divorce and the sudden, complete separation from a familiar family and a cherished dog had done more psychological harm to me than I could have possibly realized. But this was just the immediate layer of a long list of losses, rejections, and dismissals I had buried within me and hadn't properly lamented and processed.

I did not realize how traumatizing all this was for me. The loneliness felt cosmic. For better or worse, I had always dwelled among family. I took walks, watched television, ate meals, went to ball games, and shared milestone moments with kinfolk. I have spent my entire professional life deeply tethered to congregational communities, lively social groups, and many diverse circles of persons. I have planted flowers in many gardens and set down stones in many cemeteries.

There were times when I simply could not work on this project. It was too much—I've seen a great deal of the death culture now for some forty years. The freshly dug graves, the shiny caskets, the embalming rooms, the family alcoves in the funeral chapels where people in black garb sit in suffering dismay. Like many others my age or younger, I have buried my parents, many warm and intimate friends, and perhaps a thousand other people across this continent. Some of these individuals were very precious to me; they were wise and giving and grew into parental figures. I miss them terribly. They put up with my mistakes and they encouraged me and they allowed me the privilege of leading them in prayer. We wept and laughed together. One by one, they have been dropping out of sight. While my own bereavement for them is hardly comparable to what their families have endured, I have had a personal and tender stake in their journeys. I had to be professional in those crises when my insides were reeling and I would have rather been free to cry my eyes out.

My depression was the grim harvest of accumulative grief that got stuck in my soul when my father died over forty years ago. And I have experienced a series of losses and disruptions, including a very public removal from a long-standing senior position in the rabbinate, ruptured marriages, along with some deep family conflicts. I'm like you or anybody else in these categories; it's just that what I do for a living has everything to do with life and death. Grief, whether it's triggered by someone's departure or by an unresolved breakdown between a mother and a son, is the painful adhesion of human finitude.

The book was intermittently an albatross for me; it triggered *dybbuks*[40] and demons some days and through many nights. There were bad dreams derived from the embers of old memories working with the dying, the dead, and the survivors. I feel for my service colleagues—the doctors and the nurses, the police officers, and the firefighters. And the funeral managers. For all those who look through the window of human frailty. A remarkable emergency room nurse once told me, "I look for God in all the bandages, nebulizers, and stomach pumps. When I go home, I have trouble muffling the shouts and screams that pound against my ears for hours at a time. But it's what we do."

As if pushed by an advancing tornado of stored reminiscences, I relived scores of tragic events that I was a part of during the completion of this book.

I would revisit that sixteen-year-old girl who passed away before me from cystic fibrosis when I climbed up the dimly lit steps up to my apartment at night. That same night I saw a little boy named Michael,

---

40 From Jewish folklore, *dybbuk* is a malevolent spirit that enters the body of a living person and directs that person's conduct. It is believed to be the soul of a dead person and can only be exorcised by a religious ceremony.

who had just become a bar mitzvah by me in the morning atop Israel's Mount Masada, dying in the pool of a nearby kibbutz from a congenital cardiac malfunction and me having to control his shrieking parents. I saw my father's lifeless figure in every bedside of those I visited with heart disease. I heard the singing of the departed Dr. Tallisman of Cleveland (he who loved *The Music Man*) coming from his casket in the mausoleum. I heard it while I showered in my apartment and grasped the curtain in sadness. I'd play my radio at top volume while I showered or even shaved because I overheard the dead while in the bathroom or saw their faces when I woke up suddenly at night.

My dreams of my mother and father darkened and wore me out—he who disappeared too early and who left no footprints, and she who lived to a ripe age but pressed too long upon the souls of her children. In my dreams, she was hostile and did not hold out her hand. He was sad and held his head in his hands. Where I slept became a bed of pain. I'd have probing nightmares about the job I lost so many years ago. I'd be back in that city, trying to regain the position, constantly being shoved out the door again. All the pounding griefs of my otherwise fascinating life (for which I am extremely grateful) were ghoulishly released by what I secretly called my "Pandora's Book."

A therapist asked me, "What do you actually feel in this depression?"

"Loneliness," I replied immediately.

Certainly, the therapies helped, the acupuncture sessions, and the unconditional emotional assistance and unfettered availability of a few dear and trusted friends. My daughters hurt for me; they had no idea how the very lilts of their voices would bring me a surge in spirits. Surprisingly, a number of friends told me, "I've been where you are." I discovered that many people grapple with depression, particularly in the aftermath of unrealized or unresolved grief, such as grief following the death of a loved one, an ended relationship, an embroilment with a child, or losing a job.

So I was surrounded by support and freely shared of my anguish. People knew how to listen. But they couldn't move in with me or indulge my raging need for company. Nor could they fight the depression on my behalf. I resolved to bring myself back to life. Knowing that creativity is an antidote for loneliness, I sought out and accepted volunteer opportunities in the community. I became active at the local YMCA, mixing with people, taking on service projects, breathing in the life-giving laughter of day camp children as I worked out harder than ever on the treadmill. I began to regularly visit with the residents of an area nursing home. I paid attention as Holocaust survivors told me stories of their frightful and life-redeeming journeys. I heard the anguished narratives of older folks whose children had abandoned them or whose siblings did not speak to them over some petty insult or, more often, over an indignity caused by money.

I got up from the self-absorption and realized how much I learned about limits, wounded memories, and our need as mortals to lean into our grief. It became a treasury of bittersweet wisdom—about how we can't control the things that happen, but we don't have to give them control, either; about how my daughters and granddaughters and my students and friends and congregants make all the crooked spaces straight for me; about how they all fill the holes in my heart put there by my own narrative; and how they assure me that my life has not been lived for anything more important than to thank them for showing up.

This gift was on my mind when, post-depression, I went to visit an elderly lady, who had just relocated to an assisted-living facility. One of her children had phoned me and asked me to stop by. Mrs. Gordon was not adjusting well. She was dignified and alert. "I don't feel right about having other people take care of my personal needs. Imagine, not even being able to go to the bathroom by myself? My husband is gone, my mobility is gone, I haven't got so many things anymore. What do you think, is it worth it for me to continue living?"

Something or *someone* tapped me on the shoulder. Was it Charlotte Banda, the old spirit who occasionally sends me gleams of hope? Was it my father, awakening from his melancholy and transmitting me some light? I looked at Mrs. Gordon and asked, "But what *do* you have?" She thought a moment and looked out the window. There happened to be a stunning vista of Southern California mountains in the distance against a bold blue sky. "I will think about that," she answered. "Certainly I have my kids and my grandchildren and a great-grandchild on the way. I guess I should stick around and be present as long as I'm still here."

. . . .

Near the beginning of this book, I described an old custom that once prevailed among certain French Jews. You may recall that the men in some communities were guided by tradition to construct the family eating table from suitable lumber. A man would do so knowing that his coffin would one day be built from the wood of that table. In most every culture, the kitchen table has always been the epicenter of family interaction, conversations, disagreements, drama, and laughter. The true character of a man—or a woman—is revealed as relatives and guests sit with them at their table. Will he nourish them or, through inattentiveness and self-absorption, leave them spiritually hungry? What will people remember and think one day, at his funeral, when they look upon his coffin drawn, literally, from the wood of that table? What kinds of marks were left on that wood?

I thought about this ritual when I heard from a longtime friend in Cleveland named Mary Anne. She and her husband Joe had once been leading editorial executives at the *Cleveland Plain Dealer*. Mary Anne and Joe enjoyed a beloved friendship as deep as their shared reverence for writing and publishing. Mary Anne has traversed a great deal of loss in her family across the years. Then Joe died more recently, and she has grieved and rebuilt a life for herself gracefully and wisely.

Mary Anne was having a birthday and, naturally, received many kind messages. She posted the following on social media, which recalled for me the French tradition of worn wood and personal values and how grief is a great teacher, when it sends us back to bless the living:

> I so appreciate all the birthday wishes. So great to hear from friends from all stages of life, and I have certainly been through a lot of stages.
>
> Kaylie, six, said to me on my birthday, "Grandma, you have a lot of scratches on your (dining) table." I told her that table has seen a lot of events and dinners through the years. That's why I treasure that table and see on it a holiday feast, a birthday cake, glasses of wine, cat scratches, parrot bites, family reunions, and toasts to new beginnings and profound losses.
>
> So I like the scratches, and mine too, all well earned through the years.[41]

As for me, I channeled and distilled my long-running grief and emerged from the depression months before this book was completed. Grief brings with it informative distinctions; it has a way of revealing the ones who are actively on your side. My friends and I have all walked through the woods and bent many twigs together. My daughters certainly helped me cross over the bridge to peace. I learned how to be alone yet not to be lonely. I discovered that grief was not my friend but remains my necessary companion. There was no set formula for this; grief does not work well with old standard charts. But it is always defeated by love.

I remember how as I gazed into the wedding canopy where my younger daughter exchanged marriage vows with her betrothed a few years ago, all my fears floated out of me. The professional dreads, the

41 Reprinted from Facebook with permission by Mary Anne Sharkey.

generational anxieties, the clinging grudges, and the pounding griefs of this existence all vanished. Time and mortality and the insecurities disappeared beneath the river of life.

The bride was happy; she was no longer a child, and the twigs bent under her feet toward eternity. Nothing cost anything, there were no cloaked resentments in the night air, and people were momentarily at utter peace with another. The only clock we knew had its hands in the stars; the moon knew everything, looked down, and sighed.

. . . .

These are the moments when you just know there is a heaven somewhere and the best part is you don't have to struggle with what that even means. You float in these rare interludes of tender human milestones and you cross, with some of the Zoroastrian mystics, over the Chinvat Bridge into paradise.

You dance with the Hopi Indians, cotton strands in your hands, making flowers to symbolize the heavens. Your eyes sting with the Buddhist wisdom that those who live in these moments may yet bless this realm again with angelic insight.

You are at one with everything and your pockets, like the white burial shrouds of the Jews, are empty. Your heart is full and you are not afraid to die. The happiness of a child is the bridge that binds this side to the other, and there you are as you comprehend for a fleeting, delicious moment, why it is good to be born and it is okay to die.

When my other daughter was born, I felt the stirrings of creation and my own particle of partnership with it. When my father died, inexplicably and impossibly young, and we opened the earth to bury him, my mother cried like a broken vessel under the cold sun. My little sister danced among the nearby headstones and sang happy songs in defiance of the tyranny of time. Every moment like this has poured the peace into me; I know that the wine is sometimes bitter and sometimes sweet.

My much older mother wept again as I gazed into the canopy that night, smelling the nearby orange groves of central Israel and distant scent of the sea. It was not far from where I was born and it is also not far from where my parents—and all our elders—now sleep in the dust. I hear their voices from time to time, so I know that my children will one day hear mine. I don't need anybody to tell me who or what heaven is and I'm no longer afraid of death. Experience and birth and sacred promises and exceptional pain have all filled me with quiet compliance. Who can be free near a child's rapture and not know there is hope?

May you grieve well enough to honor your dead and then—as they would wish—survive and live on. And may the memories of your departed be for blessings.

Acknowledgments

· · · · · · · · · · ·

I cannot express fully the love and appreciation I carry for my daughters, Sari and Debra, and my twin granddaughters, Anora and Leela. From the lighthouse of life, I see them as shining stars on the horizon.

I wish to acknowledge my dearest and closest friends, including Professor David Miller, Robin Schulze, Rick Alter, Lynn West, and Debbie Allen, among others, who have supported me in grief and in the most joyous times of celebration.

I'm grateful for the wisdom and caring of my cousin, Rachel, my touchstone.

I'm grateful for the memory of my sweet grandmothers with whom I studied scriptural stories while literally gazing at the biblical Samarian Mountains.

I acknowledge and hail the hard work and cheerful advocacy of my editor, Nancy Schenck of Central Recovery Press, who is as joyous as she is meticulous and so very dedicated.

I am grateful for the inspiration, day in and day out, of the life and legacy of Rev. Martin Luther King Jr., of blessed memory.

Also by Ben Kamin

Stones in the Soul: One Day in the Life of an American Rabbi

*Raising a Thoughtful Teenage: A Book of
Answers and Values for Parents*

Thinking Passover: Rabbi's Book of Holiday Values

The Path of the Soul: Making Peace with Mortality

Remora: Novel of the Rabbinate

*The Spirit behind the News: On Finding God in Family,
Presidents, Baseball, Cell Phones, and Chevy Impalas*

*Nothing like Sunshine: A Story in the Aftermath
of the MLK Assassination*

Room 306: The National Story of the Lorraine Motel

My Bargain with God: The Story of Holocaust Survivor Lou Dunst

*Dangerous Friendship: Stanley Levison, Martin
Luther King Jr., and the Kennedy Brothers*

*I Don't Know What to Believe: Making
Spiritual Peace with Your Religion*